Violent Borders

*Refugees and the
Right to Move*

Reece Jones

VERSO
London • New York

This paperback edition first published by Verso 2017
First published by Verso 2016
© Reece Jones 2016, 2017

3 5 7 9 10 8 6 4

Verso
UK: 6 Meard Street, London W1F 0EG
US: 20 Jay Street, Suite 1010, Brooklyn, NY 11201
versobooks.com

Verso is the imprint of New Left Books

ISBN-13: 978-1-78478-474-4
ISBN-13: 978-1-78478-472-0 (US EBK)
ISBN-13: 978-1-78478-473-7 (UK EBK)

British Library Cataloguing in Publication Data
A catalogue record for this book is available from the British Library

The Library of Congress Has Cataloged the Hardcover Edition as Follows:

Names: Jones, Reece, author.
Title: Violent borders : refugees and the right to move / by Reece Jones.
Description: London, UK ; Brooklyn, NY : Verso, [2016] | Includes
  bibliographical references and index.
Identifiers: LCCN 2016019159 | ISBN 9781784784713 (hardback : alk. paper)
Subjects: LCSH: Emigration and immigration – Social aspects. | Emigration and
  immigration – Government policy. | Border security – Social aspects. |
  Freedom of movement – Social aspects. | Refugees – Government policy.
Classification: LCC JV6225 .J66 2016 | DDC 325 – dc23
LC record available at https://lccn.loc.gov/2016019159

Typeset in Sabon by MJ & N Gavan, Truro, Cornwall
Printed and bound by CPI Group (UK) Ltd, Croydon, CR0 4YY

Contents

Preface to the Paperback Edition

The year after I completed the original manuscript for *Violent Borders* was tumultuous. Against most expectations, the United Kingdom voted to leave the European Union, the United States elected Donald Trump president, and right-wing antimigrant nationalist political parties saw growing support around the world.

To my surprise and slight discomfort, it became clear during the fall 2016 US presidential campaign that Donald Trump and his advisors had reached a similar diagnosis of the problems of globalization that I outline in this book: borders that are open for corporations, capital, and consumer goods but closed for workers and regulators are creating dramatic inequalities in wealth and opportunity within individual countries and at a global scale. *Violent Borders* details the disastrous impacts of globalization for the majority of workers at both ends of the exchange. Workers in the United States and other wealthy countries have seen stagnating wages, the loss of benefits, and the closure of many factories. Workers in poorer countries have seen the arrival of new jobs, but they are in unregulated workplaces that offer miniscule wages, no benefits or job security, and dangerous and dirty conditions that can result in horrific tragedies like the Rana Plaza collapse in Bangladesh in 2013. Without other options, millions of people left their homes in search of better opportunities elsewhere but encountered the violence of borders as the system of citizenship and passports combined with new walls and expanded patrols to make the journey extremely fraught and perilous.

Although President Trump's campaign focused on some

of these problems caused by borders, his solutions are dia-metrically opposed to the ones I propose in this book. Trump said many times on the campaign trail, "We don't have a country if we don't have borders," and he vowed to put "America First" through limiting migration and free trade. These nationalist policies were manifested in the expansion of border security projects in the United States and in many other countries around the world. In his first months in office, Donald Trump signed executive orders withdrawing from the Transpacific Partnership free trade agreement, calling for a wall on the US-Mexico border, hiring more Border Patrol and Immigration and Customs Enforcement agents, withholding funding from sanctuary cities that chose not to inquire about the immigration status of their residents, and banning refugees and migrants from specific Muslim-majority countries. The first congressional budget of his term did not include funding for the proposed wall, but did expand it for customs and border protection and to replace older sections of the existing barrier. The leaders of countries around the world pursued similar policies in 2016 and 2017. Britain voted to leave the EU after a campaign that focused on restricting migration into the UK and regaining political and economic control from Brussels. New border walls were initiated in Algeria, Austria, Bulgaria, Estonia, Hungary, India, Jordan, Kenya, Latvia, Lithuania, Macedonia, Pakistan, Tunisia, Turkey, and the United Kingdom in Calais, France. Even Norway built a border wall in 2016.

In *Violent Borders* I propose completely different solutions to those put forward by Donald Trump, Brexit campaign-ers, and other antimigrant parties. I suggest the best way to address the inequalities of the global border regime, which allows wealth to accumulate in the hands of corporations and powerful states at the expense of workers around the world, is to remove restrictions on movement for workers and remove the barriers of state sovereignty for regulators. This would immediately reduce the number of tragic deaths at borders because people on the move would no longer need to use smugglers and take dangerous routes. It would allow workers the freedom to seek opportunities elsewhere, rather than being contained in their place of birth. By moving toward global regulations on wages, working conditions, and environmental protections, the economic playing field would be standardized and the pressure on companies to always pursue lower wages and fewer worker protections would be reduced.

Despite these seismic shifts in global politics, the core arguments of the book are unchanged and remain as relevant as ever. Freedom of movement is a fundamental human right, not something that can be restricted by a racist or nationalist government. Borders are not natural divisions between people or benign lines on a map. They are mechanisms for some groups of people to claim land, resources, and people, while fundamentally excluding other people from access to those places. They create and exacerbate inequalities and they protect the economic, political, and cultural privileges that have accrued over the past few hundred years through the spoils of colonialism, capitalism, and most recently economic globalization. Drawing a border is an inherently violent act that relies on the threat of force to support a territorial claim. As this book argues, building walls and securing borders does not stop migration but simply makes it much more dangerous. Consequently, borders continue to kill. Even with the massive amount of attention paid to the issue and the vast funds expended to stop migration, people continued to move in 2016 and the year shattered the record for the number of border deaths, with over 7,800 people losing their lives simply trying to go from one place to another.

The only corrective I would add to the text is to acknowledge that the original book does not focus on race and gender as much as it could have. The exclusionary policies that make borders so violent today are implemented in the name the citizens of America or Britain—by which their proponents really mean "white Americans" or "white Brits." There is a clear tendency for the fear of the other to be particularly pronounced when the other body is brown or black. The book makes this point, but the events of the past year have reemphasized the significant role of race in the expansion of border security and in society's ambivalence to the appalling violence borders do to the bodies of others.

Reece Jones
26 May 2017
Honolulu, HI USA

Acknowledgments

The question that drives this book, why states are often concerned with limiting the movement of the poor, was inspired by the work of James C. Scott. Scott writes, in the introduction to *Seeing Like a State*, that he began working on the book with the question of "why the state has always seemed to be the enemy of people who move around." He notes that "nomads and pastoralists (such as Berbers and Bedouins), hunter-gatherers, Gypsies, vagrants, homeless people, itinerants, runaway slaves, and serfs have always been a thorn in the side of states. Efforts to permanently settle these mobile populations (sedentarization) seemed to be a perennial state project—perennial because it so seldom succeeded." Although Scott writes that this question ended up being a road not taken for him—his book instead focuses on why mega-planning projects by states often fail—his work inspired me to investigate it here.

This book has benefited from the comments and insights of dozens of people over the three-year period in which I conceived of and wrote it. First and foremost, I want to thank my partner, Sivylay Kham Jones, and my children, Rasmey and Kiran, for their support during the research and writing process. They traveled with me to several research sites and gave me the time to write the book. Thanks also to my brother, Brent, for reading and editing the entire draft and my parents, Celia and Wally, for their support and encouragement.

My frequent collaborator, Corey Johnson, also read and commented on the entire book, provided feedback throughout the research and writing process, and traveled with me during the field research in Melilla, Spain, and Nador, Morocco. Sections of chapter 2 are derived from a coauthored paper with Corey Johnson entitled "Border Militarization and the Rearticulation of Sovereignty," which was published in the *Transactions of the Institute of British Geographers*. It is used here with permission. Jill Williams, Lynn Cochran, and John Padwick read parts of chapters at different stages of writing. Julius Paulo created the global border walls maps. Thanks to Audrea Lim and the folks at Verso for believing in this project and shepherding it to publication.

Several chapters received valuable feedback at workshops and conferences. Chapter 4 was originally presented at the Borders, Walls, and Security Conference on October 17, 2013, at the University of Quebec at Montreal. Chapter 7 was presented as part of the Presidential Dream Lecture Series at the University of Oklahoma on November 14, 2013. Chapter 2 was presented on September 26, 2014, at the Borders and Globalization Conference in Ottawa, in revised form on May 21, 2015, at the Department of Geography at the University of Oulu in Finland, and on October 15, 2015, in the International Cultural Studies Lecture Series at the East-West Center in Honolulu. Thanks to Élisabeth Vallet, Fred Shelley, Travis Gliedt, Emanuel Brunet-Jailly, Victor Konrad, Lauren Martin, and Nandita Sharma for the invitations to speak. Thanks to Oliver Belcher, Simon Dalby, Michael Dear, Anssi Paasi, Darren Purcell, William Walters, and the audiences generally for insightful questions and comments on the presentations. Thanks to Michael Eilenberg for inviting me to the Klitgården writers retreat in June 2014. The week of the midnight sun in Skagen, Denmark, proved to be a crucial period of writing and reflection that finally gave this project a direction. Thanks also to the fellow Skagen School members Zach Anderson, Erin Collins, Jason Cons, Mike Dwyer, Christian Lentz, Christian Lund, Duncan McDuie-Ra, Jonathan Padwe, and Nancy Lee Peluso for their feedback on my proposal.

This book is based on field research that was facilitated by colleagues and research assistants. Joe Heyman provided valuable advice and connections during my time in El Paso, Texas, in March 2011. Thanks to Riton Quiah for his work in Bangladesh and India in 2006 and 2007 and Namareq Younus for assistance in Palestine in 2010. John Padwick was an amazing source of knowledge about the Midlands Revolt during a research trip in May 2014. My dad and Steve Burnley were wonderful traveling partners on that trip. Mimoun Attaheri, Marcelo Di Cintio, Xavier Ferrer-Gallardo, and Said Saddiki provided useful contacts and information in Morocco and Melilla in November 2014 and March 2015.

Thanks to the International College of Seville for hosting me during my stay in Seville. Thanks also to my colleagues in the Department of Geography at the University of Hawai'i at Mānoa, who believed in this project and supported me through course releases and research funds. Mahalo! Any errors that remain are mine.

Introduction

In November 2014, I led a weekend trip to Morocco for American students studying in Spain. It was rainy on the day we took the ferry across the Strait of Gibraltar from Algeciras to Tangier. It was too wet for the first event on our itinerary, a dromedary ride, but our Moroccan guide promised to get the students on a camel at the end of the day, before we took the ferry back to Spain. My students might have imagined a journey through the vast sands of the Sahara, but the reality was three scruffy animals in a waterfront parking lot in the rundown outskirts of Tangier.

As soon as our bus, with its EU license plates, arrived at the lot, fifteen or twenty Moroccan youths, roughly the same age as the American students, surrounded the vehicle, peering underneath it. Most of the students, focused on the animals, did not even notice the commotion, but one of them thought the boys' soccer ball was stuck under the bus and bent down to try to help them find it. The Spanish driver and his Moroccan assistant tried to shoo the boys away. It quickly became apparent that the boys were trying to climb under the bus and inside the engine compartment. The driver, helpless and exasperated, gave up and got back behind the wheel. Every minute or two he honked the horn, encouraging the students to hurry up.

When the last student dismounted and boarded the bus, the assistant tried to dislodge the boys from the engine compartment at the back. The moment he disappeared inside the bus, five more boys opened the cover to the engine and held on. For the study-abroad students, safely seated inside taking

© Photo by Sivylay Jones 2016

The bus in Tangier, Morocco

cell-phone videos, this was just part of the adventure. The boys clung to the bus and a dream as we wove through traffic on the way to the port.

The port was twenty minutes away, and the knowledge that four or five boys were hanging on to the back as the bus reached 100 kilometers per hour was unsettling—not to mention the others clinging unseen to the vehicle's underside, squeezed into the wheel wells or the engine compartment. Was there anything they could hold on to that would not scorch their hands? Would a bump dislodge them? What if one of them fell and died? What would we do when we arrived at the port? Despite my sympathy for them, I was also angry that they were putting us, especially the bus driver, in this position.

The guard at the port's gate used his baton to knock the boys off the back. We disembarked, and it felt strange to walk outside knowing that human beings hidden inside the body of the bus were breathing quietly with hope. When I bent down to look underneath, nothing was visible. We showed our passports, waited in the lounge with sodas and snacks, then settled into the comfortable seats on the ferry heading back to Spain. The driver drove the bus to a holding area, where it was scanned by a massive X-ray machine on a flatbed truck. The resulting image revealed six concealed bodies.

Why did these boys take such a risk with so little chance of success? At another port, an activist told me that she had gotten to know a different group of boys who had also tried to sneak onto vehicles headed for Europe. For months, she saw the same boys every day. They kept on trying to get across; what other options did they have?

The border agents performed an extensive search, but could only locate five of the boys. Two dogs were brought in to find the final stowaway. Sniffing inside and outside of the vehicle, they located two more boys wedged inside. Seven boys total. Here is the thing: The seventh boy would have probably made it if the border agents had found all six they had seen in the original scan.

The global migration crisis

The years 2014 and 2015 were characterized by growing awareness—in policy circles, in the media, and in the public at large—of the plight of migrants worldwide.[1] Reports of hundreds dying in shipwrecks in the Mediterranean; thousands of refugees climbing over newly erected barbed-wire fences in Hungary; thousands more living in camps in Calais, France, waiting to sneak through the Chunnel to the United Kingdom; and ships full of Rohingya refugees being pushed back out to sea in Southeast Asia highlighted the global extent of the crisis. In this instance, the media coverage was not overly sensational and the data confirmed the unprecedented scale of global migration. The United Nations High Commissioner for Refugees found that 14 million people were displaced by war in 2014, the largest number in a single year since World War

II. In 2014, the UN reported 59.5 million displaced people globally, almost double the count in 2005 and the largest number ever.[2] These figures do not even consider the millions more who move for economic or environmental reasons, in search of a better life for themselves and their family.

In 2014, while my students and I were touring Morocco, over 3,500 people died attempting to make the same journey across the Mediterranean to Europe.[3] Globally, according to the International Organization for Migration, an estimated 40,000 people died attempting to cross a border between 2005 and 2014. These are not military deaths, but civilians losing their lives as they attempt to move from one place to another. Fortunately, none of the boys under our bus died that day, but what responsibility should citizens of wealthy countries feel for these deaths at borders? After centuries of state practices designed to regulate and control movement, why do so many people continue to die at the edges of modern, civilized, and democratic states?

There is a powerful idea in the media and in wealthy societies that violence at borders is inevitable when less developed, less orderly countries rub against the rich, developed states of the world. This version of borders is illustrated in US presidential candidate Donald Trump's description of migrants as "criminals, drug dealers, rapists, etc." and in TV shows such as National Geographic's *Border Wars*, which, as the title suggests, depicts the United States–Mexico border as a war zone where US Border Patrol agents are under constant assault from drug traffickers, criminals, and gangs invading the United States. In this view, continuing to harden and secure borders is necessary to contain the lawless violence on the other side; constructing walls and militarizing the border are the only options to protect the citizens of the state. The additional security practices at borders are described as virtuous actions that can protect innocent migrants from unscrupulous human traffickers who have a wanton disregard for the lives of their

4

human cargo. The European Union's response to deaths in the Mediterranean demonstrates this logic by suggesting that the problem can be solved by using military force against human traffickers, destroying their boats, and attacking their camps. This strategy is based on the assumption that the refugee situation is driven primarily by traffickers, not by conditions in the migrants' home countries or the restrictive immigration policies of states that do not provide safe and orderly systems for refugee and asylum claims.[4]

This book disputes the idea that borders are a natural part of the human world and that migration is driven primarily by traffickers and smugglers. Instead, the existence of the border itself produces the violence that surrounds it. The border creates the economic and jurisdictional discontinuities that have come to be seen as its hallmarks, providing an impetus for the movement of people, goods, drugs, weapons, and money across it. The hardening of the border through new security practices is the source of the violence, not a response to it.

States and movement

States have not always existed. Along with nations, borders, and territories, they were created to address problems of control that emerged over the past 5,000 years. This book focuses on the interactions between states and people who move around—which is just about everyone—and argues that the violence of borders today is emblematic of a broader system that seeks to preserve privilege and opportunity for some by restricting access to resources and movement for others.[5]

Far from being a new feature of the globalizing world, the movement of people has been a threat to states since the earliest ones began to collect resources in towns and cities.[6] The nomadic Mongols raided early sedentary Chinese states, whose rulers built wall after wall to keep them out.[7] The tribes of northern Britannia lived in economically unprofitable lands, so the Romans built Hadrian's Wall to consolidate their position, monitor movement in the area, and collect taxes on traders who passed through. Medieval city walls in Europe served a similar purpose: to protect resources in the event of an attack, but also to regulate and tax the movement of people in and out of the city. In the past twenty years, the United States, the European Union, and dozens of other countries have built walls on their borders to prevent the movement of people and goods into their territories.

Historically, movement restrictions were not just at borders and were not always enforced with walls. In sixteenth- and seventeenth-century England, local lords wanted to make common lands—mostly pastures and forests used by peasants for basic subsistence—more profitable in the emerging agrarian capitalist economy. They limited free movement into pastures and forests by building hedges around them and converting them into private properties, which they used as fields for commodity crops or pastures for their own sheep. In the seventeenth century, European kingdoms and city-states were faced with the problem of the movement of religious ideas, with Protestantism or Catholicism entering their lands and converting populations against the will of local rulers. After the bloody and unresolved Thirty Years' War (1618–48), which included all of the European powers and resulted in the deaths of one-quarter of the European population, the treaties of Westphalia introduced the idea of using territorial sovereignty, drawn on maps, to establish who had the right to make decisions in a particular place. In the twentieth century, with the sovereign states of Westphalia more entrenched, the movement of the poor from one state to another led to a new system of passports and visas to establish identity and citizenship and thereby restrict movement.

In addition to locating and settling the poor, these movement restrictions control and limit access to resources, not only for individuals but increasingly for other states and corporations. In the second half of the twentieth century, one of the last bastions of free movement, the high seas, was carved up at the United Nations through the creation of the Law of the Sea. Previously, coastal states only had jurisdiction within three nautical miles (5.6 km or 3.5 miles) of the coastline and could not regulate the movement of ships and other states farther off their coasts. The new agreement, which was signed in 1982 and came into force in 1994, extended coastal states' claims to resources to as far as 350 nautical miles (648 km or 403 miles) from the coast. This allows for oil extraction in deep-sea wells and for states to sign contracts for factory fishing far off their coasts. This single document extended movement restrictions to 44 percent of the ocean, which it reclassified as territorial seas, exclusive economic zones, and extended continental shelves, just as enclosure in England 400 years earlier turned common lands into private property.

The billions of dollars spent on mapping, enclosing, and bounding territories have dramatically transformed, restricted, and controlled the movement of people. Whereas 10,000 years ago most humans were migratory hunter-gatherers, today the majority of humans are born in a bounded state and live in a city, and their daily activities are monitored by agents of the state, including police, judges, and bureaucrats. The state records births and provides identity documents in the form of passports, driver's licenses, and identity cards. The state shapes knowledge through schools and media and monitors wealth through property and tax databases. Borders, walls, and documents limit movement between state territories. Each new method of locating and monitoring the actions of individuals is necessary because previous efforts continue to fail; even the restrictions of the most powerful, wealthy, and technologically advanced states are evaded on a daily basis.

When passive expressions of power such as walls, borders, or property laws fail, physical violence is often the only means left to prevent undesired movement. Some migrants are killed by border agents, but most deaths at borders occur because new enforcement technologies, from walls to drones and high-technology sensors, make the crossing much more difficult and dangerous. Migrants are funneled through the parched deserts of the southwestern United States, across the Mediterranean to Europe on unseaworthy boats, through ports in the cramped confines of shipping containers, wedged inside the engine compartments of buses, or stuffed in the trunks of cars passing through the Chunnel connecting France and the United Kingdom.

The violence of borders

The title of this book refers to multiple levels of violence at borders.[8] In addition to the visible violence borders do to the bodies of migrants, there are also other, more subtle—but also systematic—forms of violence at borders.[9] The World Health Organization's *World Report on Violence and Health* defines violence as "the intentional use of physical force or power, threatened or actual, against oneself, another person, or against a group or community, that either results in or has a high likelihood of resulting in injury, death, psychological harm, maldevelopment, or deprivation."[10] The sociologist Johan Galtung categorized these different forms as direct and structural violence: "Whereas in the first case [direct violence] these consequences can be traced to concrete persons or actors, in the second case [structural violence] this is no longer meaningful. There may not be any person who directly harms another person in the structure. The violence is built into the structure and shows up as unequal power and consequently unequal life chances."[11]

More recently, geographers James Tyner and Joshua Inwood suggest that although there are different forms of violence, the distinction between direct and structural violence elides responsibility for the action.[12] Instead they recommend that all of these forms of violence should be highlighted and considered within their geographic and temporal contexts in order to bring to light who carries out the violence, how it is perpetrated, and why.

The case for understanding borders and resource enclosures as fundamentally violent draws on these broader and more nuanced definitions of violence. The overt violence of border guards and border security infrastructure is only one aspect of the violence borders inflict on people and on the environment. The second form is the use of force or power—threatened or actual—that increases the chances of injury, death, or deprivation. For example, the construction of walls and the deployment of thousands of additional Border Patrol agents at the US–Mexico border has prevented easy crossings in urban areas like El Paso and San Diego and funneled migrants to harsh and dangerous deserts, where thousands have died. The third form is the threat of violence necessary to limit access to land or to a resource through an enclosure—for instance, the threat of punishment for trespassing on private land or of arrest for not possessing the proper identity papers. The fourth form is the violence borders do to the economic well-being of people around the world. This is a collective, structural violence that deprives the poor of access to wealth and opportunities through the enclosure of resources and the bordering of states. The fifth form of violence is the direct harm borders do to the environment, including through the construction of walls, the deployment of security personnel, and the use of surveillance technologies. Moreover, borders create separate jurisdictions that allow the ideology of resource extraction to become pervasive by preventing uniform environmental regulations. By allowing each country to put the well-being of the people inside its borders before the well-being of the world as a whole, borders fracture the regulation of the environment and prevent meaningful action to combat climate change. These other forms of violence at borders are not as obvious as migrant deaths, but they are a direct outcome of a political system that seeks to control access to resources and limit movement around the world. Taken together, borders should be seen as inherently violent, engendering systematic violence to people and the environment.

Although the technologies states use today to control resources, land, and people—drones, heat sensors, smart borders, global positioning systems, remote sensing images, biometric passports—would have been unimaginable for ancient rulers, the underlying problem of people who move would have been all too familiar to them. Why is movement consistently a problem, for ancient rulers and modern states alike? How have rulers and the state responded to this problem historically? Why is the response so violent today? This book tells the story of the conflicting impulse of movement and of settlement, of searching for something new and of protecting what you already have. *Violent Borders* theorizes movement and fixity as a conflict between the desire for freedom and the desire for control, between people who move around and people who want them to stay in place.

In the first half of the book, I delve into the causes and consequences of the global migration crisis. The first chapter asks why the European Union, which was once at the forefront of opening internal borders to free movement, became the locus of the current crisis, as more than 23,000 people lost their lives at its borders from 2005 to 2015. The second chapter turns to the United States' border with Mexico to illustrate how borders have been transformed from lines on a map that depicted states' territorial claims into deadly spaces of violent security practices. The final chapter of the first section visits borders around the world in order to make the case that the violence of borders is not limited to "Western" states like the European Union and United States, but is inherent to the practice of making borders. Collectively, these chapters tell the stories of people who have experienced the violent reality of borders and consider how these encounters shape their lives.

The second half of the book argues that other types of boundaries, such as private property and resource enclosures on the land and at sea, are long-term and widespread parts of how states maintain privileges by restricting movement. Chapter 4 argues that movement restrictions at borders today are part of a long-term effort to control the movement of the poor, which has its roots in slavery, vagrancy, and poor laws. Chapter 5 begins with the Midlands Revolt of 1607—the largest peasant uprising in the history of England—by telling the improbable story of "Captain Pouch," who convinced his followers that the contents of his magical pouch would protect them from all harm as he led a revolt against the enclosure of common land into private property. The chapter continues through the enclosure of land into state territory and the enclosure of the oceans into exclusive economic zones with the implementation of the Law of the Sea. The sixth and seventh chapters unearth the role borders play in perpetuating inequality and damaging the environment. Chapter 6 begins with the horrific story of the Rana Plaza factory collapse in Bangladesh, which killed more than 1,100 people, in order to draw a connection between the slave-like working conditions in many poor countries and the existence of movement restrictions at borders. The seventh chapter connects the global failure to address issues like climate change to the role borders play in dividing the world into separate sovereign territories that place the interests of citizens above the interests of human beings generally. The final chapter makes the case that the deaths of migrants in the global migration crisis require us to reconsider the damage that militarized borders and resource enclosures do to humanity and the earth.

Chapter 1

The European Union:
The World's Deadliest Border

The Spanish city of Melilla, a crescent of sandy beaches and modernist architecture nestled on the rocky Mediterranean coast, is a fortified garrison that has survived sieges and invasions since it was founded. The ancient city is mentioned in 2,000-year-old Roman geographical texts and was acquired by Spain in 1497, at the end of the reconquest of the Iberian Peninsula from the Moors. Over the ensuing centuries, Melilla was reinforced with city walls and troop deployments to protect it from multiple attempts to retake it. What sets Melilla apart from Seville, Granada, and other reconquered Spanish cities is that it is not on the Iberian Peninsula. Melilla and its sister city, Ceuta, are across the Strait of Gibraltar, the only outposts of Spain—and by extension the European Union—on the North African coast. As the only land borders between the European Union and African countries, both Melilla and Ceuta have become beacons for migrants attempting to set foot in the EU and apply for asylum.[1] Today Melilla still resembles a fortified garrison, but now the walls, fences, and security personnel are in place as a bulwark against not military invasion but the movement of refugees and migrants.

I traveled to Melilla and Nador, a bustling port city of approximately 300,000 on the other side of the Moroccan border, in March 2015 to see the unfolding migration crisis firsthand. After visiting the fence complex and the old market, I settled into a chair at an open-air café, beside several fruit vendors with heaping piles of strawberries on carts, for a glass of sweet Moroccan mint tea. Isaac, a Ghanaian migrant, heard me speaking English with a colleague and approached to ask for some money. His wife, Gifty, stayed in the street with their newborn son Samuel strapped to her back, while their four-year-old son Prince, in torn ragged clothes, wandered back and forth between them.[2] In 2012 the family had left Ghana, where they faced the options of working in low-wage subsistence agriculture or grinding out an existence in the slums of Accra. They had traveled through West Africa before arriving in Nador, expecting to spend a short time in the city before continuing their journey into Europe.

Nador, like many Moroccan cities, is vibrant and contradictory, with gleaming new sedans passing street vendors, hawkers, and farmers bringing their crops to market by oxcart. The city leaders have ambitions of making Nador a low-cost tourist destination and are constructing a long seafront promenade with benches under palm trees. On the outskirts of the urban core, beyond the future tourists' gaze, new apartment blocks are going up haphazardly to house workers. Whether or not the European tourists eventually arrive, Nador is already a popular destination for migrants from across Africa and the Middle East who gather to slip through the EU checkpoint with false documents, climb over the fence in the early morning hours, or catch a boat headed for the Spanish mainland, tantalizingly close on the other side of the Mediterranean.

Refugees from Syria typically go through the checkpoint because their appearance matches the residents of Nador, who have identity cards that allow them to enter Melilla legally for the day. Migrants from West Africa, like Isaac and Gifty, gather in camps in the forests on Mount Gurugu, the peak that looms above Nador and Melilla, before attempting to jump the Spanish fences in large groups to ensure that at least a few make it through before border guards locate them and send them back to Morocco. Spain began to construct fences and barricades on the boundaries of Melilla in 1993, and they have been redesigned and expanded multiple times. The current wall complex is made up of three fences, the tallest of which is six meters (20 feet), all heavily reinforced to prevent them from being knocked down by a truck. The Spanish Guardia Civil, in older white trucks with green doors, patrol the roads along the edge of the fences, looking for anything out of place. If migrants make it over all three fences and set foot in the European Union, Spain is obligated to hear their asylum requests and provide them shelter. However, if they only make it over the first or second fence, they have not yet set foot in the EU and can be returned to Morocco. This is why there are often images in the news of dozens of migrants perched on the fences, with Guardia Civil waiting for them below. The migrants stuck on the fence have been stopped, but they are waiting to see if an opportunity to sneak past the guards might still present itself.

© José Palazón Osma 2016

The border fence in Melilla, Spain

In the past five years, as the number of migrants attempting to enter Melilla has continued to grow, Spain has contracted with Morocco to transfer much of the work of guarding the border to the Moroccan side. The European Union signed a joint immigration agreement with Morocco in 2013, which provides funding in exchange for help from the Moroccan authorities in preventing migrants from reaching the Melilla fence. While the Spanish fence is sometimes termed a "humanitarian fence" because it does not use barbed wire or razor wire, the new Moroccan fence, built with EU funds in 2015, is decidedly not: it consists of rolls of concertina wire wrapped with barbed wire, with sentry posts every hundred meters. In February 2015, a few weeks before my visit, the Moroccan authorities had carried out a major operation to locate and detain migrants in the areas surrounding Melilla. They cleared the major migrant camps on Mount Gurugu, detained hundreds of migrants, and burned their structures and supplies. They moved the migrants to detention facilities across Morocco, but predominantly in the south, far from the edges of the European Union. It was unclear whether Morocco would eventually release the migrants or deport them.

Isaac and Gifty had avoided the raids on the migrant camps by living by themselves. They had never attempted to jump the fence—it would have been too difficult with small children —and were instead looking to travel to Europe by boat. They had already made three attempts, but had been pushed back by the Moroccan coast guard before they even made it away from the coastline. Their infant was born while they were living in the forests on the hills above Nador. They spend their days wandering through the city looking for money and food, relying on the kindness of the local residents to help them get by while they wait for another opportunity to travel to Europe. Isaac sat and chatted with us for a while. He was articulate and friendly, but had a weary look in his eyes. When

I asked him if he ever considered going back to Ghana, he said no. "We have been gone for three years. What would I say to my family if they saw me?" While we talked, their son Prince wandered off and came back a moment later with a proud smile and a large strawberry in his hand. A kind Moroccan fruit vender had given it to him.

Although Isaac, Gifty, Prince, and Samuel remain stuck in the bleak existence of unwanted migrants in Morocco, at least they still have their lives. Many other migrants who do manage to find their way onto a boat are not as lucky. The International Organization for Migration reports that more than 23,700 migrants have died attempting to enter the EU since 2004.[3] The death rate is increasing, with more than 3,500 deaths in 2014 and 3,770 in 2015.[4] Globally, more than half the deaths at borders in the past decade occurred at the edges of the EU, making it by far the most dangerous border crossing in the world.

The European migration crisis

This was not supposed to be the story of borders in the EU in the era of globalization.[5] Through the 1990s, the dominant media narrative was the removal of borders in Europe. The Berlin Wall fell in 1989 and in the early 1990s the Iron Curtain lifted as the Soviet Union collapsed. Former Soviet states became independent and many transitioned to democracy and open capitalist economies. In 1995, the Schengen Area, named for the small town in Luxembourg where the agreement was signed, was established, with visa-free movement through internal borders in Europe. By 2014, twenty-six countries were participating, including EU nonmembers Iceland, Liechtenstein, Norway, and Switzerland. These changes in Europe seemed to symbolize the possibility that globalization might create a borderless world.

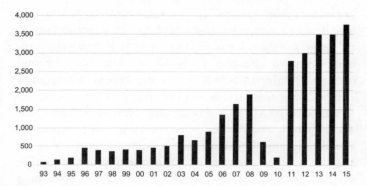

Migrant deaths at the edges of the European Union. Data from International Organization for Migration Missing Migrants Project (missingmigrants.iom.int) and Brian and Laczko, Fatal Journeys.

The reality is that EU borders were not removed in the 1990s, but simply moved to different locations. As internal border restrictions were loosened in the Schengen Area, more focus was placed on the external boundaries of the European Union at the Mediterranean and on its eastern edges.[6] Individual countries continue to have primary responsibility for border enforcement, but a new agency, Frontex, was founded in 2005 to coordinate these border patrols and ensure security across the EU.[7] New states wanting to join the Schengen Area must first demonstrate the security of their external borders, particularly at airports and in their visa requirements. The most significant change in the Mediterranean region over the past decade has been the militarization of border enforcement.[8] Even within the European Union, the ideal of free internal movement is under threat. Denmark briefly instituted border controls in 2011; in 2015 many countries, including Austria, France, and Germany, reinstated border checkpoints on internal EU borders.

Most of the recent attention to the migration issue has focused on the war in Syria, but thousands of migrants died at the European Union's borders years before that war even began: 1,650 people in 2007 and 1,900 in 2008. Despite the large numbers of deaths for over a decade, the issue only registered as a blip on the global agenda, in part due to the invisibility of bodies lost at sea. The 2013 tragedy at Lampedusa, a small Italian island that is the closest EU island to the coast of Africa, began to raise awareness. More than 500 migrants, mostly from Eritrea, Ghana, and Somalia, had boarded a smuggler's small fishing boat and set out from the coast of Libya toward Europe.⁹ After two days at sea, on the third of October, when it was less than half a kilometer (a third of a mile) off the Lampedusa coastline, the boat encountered engine trouble. Most of the migrants could not swim. They could see lights on the island and tried to signal for help. At 6 A.M., someone on the boat set fire to a blanket in order to attract the attention of another ship, but the fire spread. All of the passengers moved to a safe section of the boat, but the weight on one side capsized it and sent them all into the cold Mediterranean. The people on the deck mostly survived, but those below, including many children, died. The final count of people who lost their lives in the shipwreck will never be known, but more than 350 died. Local fishers and the Italian coast guard rescued 155. In the funeral ceremony Italian authorities held on Lampedusa, the tiny coffins of the children each had a stuffed animal placed on top. Their parents' coffins were each adorned with a single rose. The bodies that were not recovered lay in a watery grave. Only a few days later, another ship with migrants from Eritrea and Somalia sank in the same area, killing thirty-four people.

In August and September 2015, the violence of the borders of the EU burst onto the international news through a series of visually shocking stories. The first was the discovery of seventy-one bodies in an abandoned truck on the side of a highway in Austria. In contrast to bodies lost at sea, these migrants were already well within the boundaries of the EU and their deaths could not be ignored. This was followed by Hungary's efforts to secure its border with Serbia to prevent migrants from passing through on their way to Germany. The Hungarian government built a razor-wire fence on its border, which resulted in images of women and children pushing their way through the dangerous fence. Then it closed the main train station in Budapest, stranding thousands of migrants, who slept on the platforms and in the lobby. After several days camped at the station, more than 10,000 people set off on a 500-kilometer (310-mile) march to reach Germany, which produced powerful images that evoked marches in the US South against segregation and in India against British colonialism. The most shocking image, however, was the photograph of three-year-old Aylan Kurdi's dead body washed up on a Turkish beach. The innocent child lying facedown in the sand in bright red-and-blue clothing made it impossible to ignore the plight of refugees fleeing the war in Syria. Suddenly, the decade-long issue of deaths at the EU border became global news.

The year 2014, the latest year for which data are available, was characterized by the most people displaced by war in a single year since World War II (14 million) and the largest total displaced population in recorded history (59.5 million).[10] All indications are that even more people were displaced in 2015. Many of the migrants arriving in Europe were leaving war-ravaged Syria, Iraq, and Afghanistan, but there were also large numbers of migrants from Ukraine, Eritrea, and West Africa. The civil war in Syria has raged since 2011 and the conflict crossed into Iraq in 2014 as the Islamic State consolidated its authority over a territory with more than 10 million inhabitants. From 2011 to 2015, 4 million Syrians fled the country. The war in Ukraine displaced 1.3 million people within the country and an additional 867,000 fled across its borders. Another large group of migrants come from Eritrea, where a 2015 UN investigation accused the government of President Isaias Afwerki of crimes against humanity, including torture, extrajudicial kill-ings, forced labor, and sexual violence.[11] The migration crisis in Europe in 2014 and 2015 was not singularly defined by people fleeing war. Like Isaac and Gifty, many migrants from West African countries such as Cameroon, Ghana, Nigeria, and Senegal move primarily for economic reasons.

At the borders of the European Union—and the United States, for that matter—it is difficult to classify all of the people arriving under general categories like migrant, refugee, and asylum seeker. *Refugee* is a category created through the United Nations Convention on Refugees; it initially only applied to European refugees after World War II, but was revised in 1967 to remove the geographic and temporal limi-tations. The convention categorizes a refugee as someone who, "owing to well-founded fear of being persecuted for reasons of race, religion, nationality, membership of a particular social group or political opinion, is outside the country of his nation-ality and is unable or, owing to such fear, is unwilling to avail himself of the protection of that country."[12]

The category is a product of the state system of bounded territories because the primary action that a refugee has taken is crossing a border. The definition excludes most people who move, because poverty and environmental changes are not included. The poor, including Isaac and Gifty, are considered voluntary migrants.

Although there are problems with how the refugee system is organized, it does oblige receiving countries to provide basic care for the people who make claims and to consider their applications for refugee or asylum status. The European Union instituted a shared asylum policy in 2004 through the Dublin Regulations, which require applicants to request asylum in the first EU country they enter. Once a person makes the claim, their fingerprints are taken, and they are placed into a holding facility; provided food, shelter, and basic health care; and given a three-month temporary visa that allows them to move around while their claim is considered. There were 626,000 asylum applications in the European Union in 2014, 33 percent more than 2013 and an increase of over 300 percent from the number of applications in 2006. Through the first three quarters of 2015, there had already been 805,000 asylum applications.[13]

The Dublin procedure is meant to standardize asylum rules across the European Union, but each country retains the right to adjudicate asylum applications. Migrants are keenly aware that some countries are more migrant-friendly and much more likely to approve an asylum request. This leads migrants to avoid providing their fingerprints in less desirable destinations by burning their fingers, covering them with glue or plastic, or avoiding detection even though they have already reached the EU. In 2015, the Dublin protocols broke down as Hungary, Italy, and other countries on the edges of the European Union stopped taking fingerprints in order to avoid dealing with migrants who did not want to remain there anyway.

Syrian migrants' asylum requests are very likely to succeed due to the political and religious violence they are fleeing. In the third quarter of 2015, 98 percent of Syrian applicants were granted asylum in the European Union. West African economic migrants are much less likely to be given asylum. For example, in the same quarter of 2015, 76 percent of requests from Ghana were rejected. Many West African migrants choose to leave the holding facilities before their hearings and remain in the European Union without papers. They face a life of scraping by on the margins of society. In the best-case scenario, they find work through networks of migrants, washing dishes or cleaning buildings late at night. More likely they will join the throngs of migrants selling knockoff purses in the tourist areas and shopping districts of Barcelona, Paris, or Rome while keeping a wary eye out for the police.

One positive outcome of the current crisis is the consensus that more needs to be done to help one class of mobile people: refugees. In July 2015, the news agency Al Jazeera announced that it would no longer use the term *migrant* due to its negative connotations, and would instead use only *refugee*. As the crisis unfolded, the hashtag #refugeeswelcome was used on social media and to adorn banners at European football matches. The president of the European Commission, Jean-Claude Juncker, proposed that the European Union should accept 160,000 refugees. US president Barack Obama announced that the United States would accept 10,000 Syrian refugees.

Although the #refugeeswelcome movement and these countries' decisions to accept more refugees are positive developments, they also highlight the persistent exclusion inherent in border regimes and state-defined identity categories. The first problem is that the global system of borders gives individual countries discretion over refugee decisions, which allows most countries to accept too few refugees and some to avoid accepting any. Israeli prime minister Benjamin Netanyahu said Israel could not accept Syrian refugees because it is "a very small country that lacks demographic and geographic depth." Middle Eastern countries such as Qatar, Saudi Arabia, and the United Arab Emirates have not accepted any Syrian refugees.[14] Although the United States and European Union did offer to take in migrants, the number seeking asylum exceeds these new quotas by a factor of ten. For many migrants, this means dropping out of the asylum process and choosing to live without documents on the streets of Europe.

The second problem with #refugeeswelcome is that it relies on the assumption that other migrants who do not fit the limited definition of a refugee are not welcome. In the current system, a refugee fleeing political persecution is more legitimate than a migrant fleeing a life in a filthy, crowded, disease-ridden, and dangerous slum where the only option is to work long hours in a sweatshop for very low wages. Focusing only on the limited, state-defined term *refugee* renders other categories of migrants, who are moving for economic or environmental reasons, as undeserving of help or sympathy.

Who is to blame?

The crisis at the European Union's borders resulted in substantial debate about who bears responsibility for the increasing numbers of migrants and the high numbers of deaths. The European Union has primarily settled on a deterrence policy that makes crossing its borders difficult in order to dissuade migrants from attempting the trip. This also places the blame on smugglers.[15] As easier routes close, migrants continue to look for alternative routes into Europe.[16] A decade ago, the primary routes were through Spain, at Melilla and Ceuta; across the Strait of Gibraltar; and, more dangerously, across the Atlantic to the Canary Islands. Frontex, the EU-wide border agency established in 2005, began operations named "Gate of Africa," "Indalo," and "Hera" that target migration in Spain and Morocco.

After the civil war in Libya, the lack of a strong central government there allowed smugglers to shift operations to the central Mediterranean, with boats headed towards Lampedusa, Malta, and the Italian mainland. These routes have been targeted for enforcement through new Frontex missions named "Hermes," "Nautilus," and "Triton." In 2015, as hundreds of thousands of people fled the war in Syria, the main routes moved farther east, from Turkey through Greece and the Balkans to Hungary. The number of migrants crossing the Aegean Sea between Turkey and Greece increased tenfold from 2014 to 2015, to over 853,000.[17] Frontex monitors the eastern Mediterranean through operations "Poseidon" and "Aeneas." Austria, Bulgaria, Greece, and Hungary also began building fences on their borders. In December 2015, the European Union reached a three-billion-euro agreement with Turkey to limit migration; Turkey instituted new visa requirements for Syrians. In February 2016, Austria and its neighboring Balkan countries reached an agreement to severely restrict migrants from gaining access to the edges of the European Union.[18] Finally, the European Union is investing in information-sharing systems that integrate the satellites, sensors, and personnel of the member states. These include Eurosur, an information-sharing platform for border enforcement in the Mediterranean, and Sistema de Vigilancia Exterior (SIVE), a Spanish program to coordinate surveillance data.

These operations and data-gathering practices suggest that the European Union monitors the sea very carefully for vessels and is aware of most migrant boats traveling from the coast of Africa. However, because officials do not want to encourage additional migration by rescuing people outside the territorial waters of EU states, they often do not intervene until the boats reach shore or are very clearly in distress.[19] Amnesty International accused Greece in 2015 of pushing migrant boats back to sea in order to avoid dealing with them. "This is an ongoing situation that has been taking place on the Greece–Macedonia border, the Greece–Turkey border, and the Italian sea border," said Gauri van Gulik, Amnesty's deputy Europe director for the European Union and Balkans teams. "It is always illegal to push them back to where they came from."[20]

Several EU member states oppose any rescue operations for migrant ships in the Mediterranean. Lady Joyce Anelay, a British Foreign Ministry official, explained that "we do not support planned search and rescue operations in the Mediterranean" because they are "an unintended 'pull factor,' encouraging more migrants to attempt the dangerous sea crossing and thereby leading to more tragic and unnecessary deaths."[21] The logic behind this position is that if migrants know the European Union will rescue their ships, many more will make the trip. If the crossing is dangerous and thousands

of people die en route, it will discourage others from tryii.
reach Europe.

The first problem with this approach is that it assumes
all migrants have the luxury of deciding whether or not to
move. Many, if not most, do not have a choice. It also ignores
the fact that the trip has already been dangerous for over a
decade, which appears to have had no impact on the decisions
of later migrants to attempt the crossing. Indeed, more people
are coming, not fewer. This reality is captured in the powerful
poem "Home" by British Somali poet Warsan Shire:

> you have to understand,
> that no one puts their children in a boat
> unless the water is safer than the land
> [...]
> no one leaves home until home is a sweaty voice in your ear
> saying-
> leave,
> run away from me now
> i dont know what i've become
> but i know that anywhere
> is safer than here.[22]

In addition to discouraging migrants by making the trip more
dangerous, the European Union has blamed much of the crisis
on smugglers and human traffickers, whose actions put the
migrants' lives at grave risk. "European Union naval operations
in the Horn of Africa have successfully fought piracy—and a
similar initiative must be developed to effectively fight against
human trafficking in the Mediterranean," writes Matteo Renzi,
the Italian prime minister, in an op-ed in the *New York Times*.
"Trafficking vessels should be put out of operation. Human
traffickers are the slave traders of the 21st century, and they
should be brought to justice."[23] Undoubtedly, smugglers are
operating to make money, not to make a political stand against
borders or to help desperate people in need. However, focusing

on the smugglers obscures the role that EU border policy and enforcement play in increasing deaths. "Rather than mitigating the critical emergency in the Central Mediterranean," argues political geographer Timothy Raeymaekers, "its perpetuation at a subjective, human level has become a key element in the justification of a forceful border regime that is officially aimed at curbing irregular migration but which, through its effects, enhances a system of interests and relationships that has almost become an end in itself."[24]

If there was a humane and orderly way for migrants to enter the European Union, they would not choose the dangerous, violent option provided by the smugglers. The International Organization for Migration suggests that "the relatively low number of migrant deaths before 1990 may be related to the fact that it used to be much easier to reach Europe by regular means, even in the absence of official government authorization to immigrate."[25] Prior to 1974, for example, France allowed migrants to come and go freely. Spain allowed North Africans to enter freely until 1991.

Smugglers tend to take good care of their human cargo if there is a payoff for delivering them alive, but the journey across the Mediterranean is the last stage of the trip, when all of the money has already been gathered. Furthermore, the smugglers do not expect to get the boats back at the end of the journey. Consequently, the boats are of very low quality, the engines are old, there is little shelter or shade, there is the minimum amount of fuel, and there are often no navigational devices. There is little food or water because the space is reserved for more people. The boats are typically captained by one of the migrants, because if a smuggler went, they would be caught. The results are predictable: leaking ships, navigational errors, broken motors, and not enough fuel, all of which leads to hypothermia, heat stroke, starvation, and drowning.[26] Frontex has estimated that one out of every four people who attempt to enter Europe by boat dies en route.[27]

The structural violence of borders

The European migration crisis demonstrates the structural violence of the global border regime, as the hardening of borders and the closing down of migration routes makes movement extremely dangerous for the majority of the people in the world. However, as the crisis unfolded in the summer of 2015, policy makers worked to limit the geographic and temporal scope of the discussion by focusing on the war in Syria and the migrants fleeing that conflict. The result was a constrained policy response that legitimized refugees from Syria while other migrants, classified as economic or voluntary migrants, were represented as taking advantage of the Syrian refugee situation to sneak into Europe. Non-Syrian migrants were not welcome and were the primary targets of refugee status checks at the external boundaries of the European Union and through the imposition of internal border checks by Austria, France, Germany, and several other EU states. British prime minister David Cameron flew to a refugee camp in the Beqaa Valley of Lebanon in September 2015 to announce a program through which the United Kingdom will accept Syrian refugees, but only those who go to camps in neighboring countries such as Jordan, Lebanon, or Turkey, not those who make the trip to Europe on their own. Viktor Orbán, the Hungarian prime minister, went further, arguing that Syrian refugees who make it to the EU on their own are not legitimate refugees because they pass through a number of safe countries on the way.

The focus on a limited set of Syrian refugees was politically prudent. It demonstrated that EU leaders were taking the situation seriously and were acting to help refugees in need while simultaneously denying any obligation to migrants from any other place. Moreover, framing the movement of people through the Mediterranean and Aegean as a human-trafficking issue—and by extension blaming their deaths on malevolent traffickers—hides the role played by EU immigration policies. The hardening of the European Union's borders, the militarization of enforcement, and the lack of safe routes for migrants is obscured; the blame is shifted squarely onto smugglers, who operate without consideration for the lives of their cargo, and onto migrants, who still decide to make the dangerous trip.[28]

For many migrants, there is no real choice. For some, staying means enduring the violence of the Islamic State or risking their lives in a civil war. For others, it means living in a slum without access to water, electricity, or any job opportunities that would allow them to carve out a better life. During the great nineteenth-century migration, millions of European migrants faced similar economic hardships and made their way to new homes in search of better opportunities for their families in Australia, Canada, New Zealand, South Africa, and the United States. The Ghanaian migrants Isaac, Gifty, Prince, and Samuel, and millions more people like them, have no such opportunity.

These broader questions should not be lost in the specific details of how European borders are enforced or whether the refugee quotas of individual countries are sufficient. There is a larger systemic issue at stake. The true source of the crisis is that movement restrictions at borders continue to allow states to contain the poor and protect the wealth and privilege of their populations. Until free and safe movement is available to all, the European Union and wealthy countries will live with the uncomfortable reality that, because of their exclusionary border policies, dead babies will occasionally wash up on their beaches.

Chapter 2

The US–Mexico Border:
Rise of a Militarized Zone

Fifteen-year-old Sergio Hernandez Guereca and three teenage friends ran across the trickle of water in the concrete riverbed that is the Rio Grande, which marks the United States–Mexico border, on a cloudy, hot June day in 2010. The river, which runs between the urban sprawls of El Paso and Juárez, is only centimeters deep and fifteen meters wide at the border, because the United States diverts most of the water into a canal before it reaches Mexico. Above the boys, on the Paso del Norte Bridge, thousands of people from Juárez inched along on foot for two to three hours before reaching the customs agents on the US side. The audacity of the boys' run, in broad daylight in one of the most heavily patrolled spots along the entire US–Mexico border, roused the bored pedestrians on the bridge above into surprised conversation. Several turned on their cell-phone cameras to record the brazen act. The videos and the searing images of the aftermath momentarily flooded the media, with channels from CNN to Univision showing the footage.

Exactly what Sergio and his friends had in mind is unclear. Even at their young ages, they had to know that an agent would arrive within seconds of their shoes getting wet. Maybe they were a diversion for some other crossing nearby, or had a small package to drop for a smuggler, or, as their families would suggest later, were just doing something stupid to get their adrenaline pumping. They were teenage boys, after all.

Predictably, as soon as they reached the fence on the US side, they were forced to retreat. Border Patrol agent Jesus Mesa Jr.

ran in from the north with his gun already drawn. Sergio and two other boys easily evaded Mesa and jogged back across to the Mexican side. The fourth boy, perhaps seeing something in Mesa's eyes, put his hands up and was detained. Sergio and his two friends regrouped on the Mexican side. Seeing their fourth friend detained, they picked up rocks and threw them at Agent Mesa. The detained boy fell to the ground; Agent Mesa dragged him by his shirt collar a few meters toward the Rio Grande, keeping his gun pointed into Mexico at the boys, who were at least twenty or thirty meters away.

Sitting in an empty Catholic church in El Paso a few months later, María Luisa, a sprightly and energetic eighty-year-old woman who resides in El Paso but regularly travels across the bridge to visit family in Juárez, explained to me what she saw happen next.[1] "It was such a long distance," she said exasperatedly, using her hands to point to either side of the cavernous chapel. "The Border Patrol was here, the boy was there. It was so far apart. How can you compare a man who has been trained to aim, shoot, and kill—who has been trained to kill—and this young boy, with rocks?"

Agent Mesa fired twice across the border into Mexico. *Pop, pop.* Then a brief pause, followed by another *pop*. Pedestrians on the bridge gasped and screamed. "*Idiota,*" one woman said. Sergio staggered a few meters and fell beside the pylon of a railroad bridge. In the photos, the pool of blood around the wound in Sergio's head is dried and congealed on the concrete riverbed.

A few months after the shooting, I toured the border with a Latino American public relations officer with the Border Patrol. It was a hot day, so when we reached the site of the shooting, he parked the green-and-white Border Patrol truck in the shade of the Paso del Norte Bridge. For most of the visit he was gregarious, enthusiastically explaining the new surveillance technologies along the border and showing me the border fence, which, he emphasized, had a clever design that allowed small animals to slip through but prevented the movement of migrants. After he gave me a few details about the shooting of Sergio Guereca, we sat in the truck and surveyed the scene under the bridge in silence. The radio crackled with reports of a tripped sensor that agents needed to investigate; a man walked casually along the Mexican side of the river, shadowed by a Border Patrol truck on the US side; and the pedestrians above us waited their turn in the long queue. There was no remaining evidence of what had happened to Sergio there only a few months before. After a moment or two, he put the truck back in gear, glanced out the window, and said in a resigned and defensive tone, "Rocks are a deadly weapon." We headed back to the Border Patrol headquarters, where he offered me a coffee before I left.

Sergio and his friends encountered a very different US—Mexico border than the one that was originally established in the 1840s at the end of the Mexican—American War, or even the one that existed when they were born in the 1990s. The changes at the edges of the United States—and the violent consequences for migrants—are emblematic of a global change in how borders are patrolled.[2] For most of the twentieth century, borders were lines on maps that were only heavily guarded when states were at war with their neighbors. A few examples of war borders remain. The border between North and South Korea is heavily militarized, with both sides poised to defend against an invasion from the other side. Similarly, the Line of Control that marks the boundary between India and Pakistan in the disputed territory of Kashmir, which both states claimed after the partition of the subcontinent in 1947, has an extensive military presence and there are occasional skirmishes between the two forces. Despite these conspicuous exceptions, however, for most of the twentieth century this type of militarized border was rare. Most countries did not invest heavily in border security infrastructure because it was expensive, ineffective against military invasion (a plane or missile can fly right over and a tank can plow through a wall), and unnecessary in the United Nations era, when most states respected the sovereign authority of neighboring states. Most borders looked more like the US–Canada border, with customs and passport checkpoints at border crossings, but long stretches in between these official points that were open and mostly unguarded. The United States is not worried that Canada will invade across its northern border. The border marks the edges of different political and economic systems, not contentious territorial disputes.

Over the past thirty years, many borders have been transformed into militarized security spaces through increased funding, deployments of additional border guards, and the construction of walls and surveillance infrastructure. The new US–Mexico border that took the life of Sergio Guereca is a microcosm of this global change. The hardening of the US–Mexico border has resulted in both direct and structurally violent outcomes for migrants; as the easiest crossing points are closed, migrants choose to put their lives in the hands of smugglers in order to take ever more dangerous routes across the border. The difference from the militarized borders in Korea or South Asia is that the militarization of the US–Mexico border is not in response to a military threat from Mexico: it is focused entirely on preventing the movement of civilians.

The border

The current route of the US–Mexico border was established in 1848 and 1853 with the signing of the Treaty of Guadalupe Hidalgo and the Gadsden Purchase at the end of the Mexican–American War.[3] The expansionary war inaugurated the idea that the Anglo-Saxon people of America had a manifest destiny to expand the United States across the continent, from sea to shining sea. It resulted in the third-largest land acquisition in the history of the United States, after the Louisiana Purchase of 1803, which gave the US 2.14 million square kilometers (827,000 square miles) and the 1867 purchase of Alaska from Russia (1.5 million square kilometers, 586,00 square miles). The treaty of Guadalupe Hidalgo transferred about half of Mexico's territory (1.36 million square kilometers, 525,000 square miles) to the United States, including large sections of US states in the Southwest: Arizona, California, Colorado, Nevada, New Mexico, Utah, and Wyoming. At the time, these arid and sparsely populated lands were still not firmly under the control of the Mexican state. They included a population of 200,000 Native Americans (or, as the treaty refers to them, "savage tribes"), and 100,000 former Mexican citizens. Ninety percent of the Mexican citizens decided to become US citizens; the rest relocated to the Mexican side of the new border.

In the years after the war, the US—Mexico border was marked on maps but not necessarily on the ground. The framers of the treaty recognized that much of the land under discussion was unknown and, "in order to preclude all difficulty in tracing upon the ground the limit separating Upper from Lower California," they opted to draw a straight line on the map that would need to be located on the ground later, through a joint Mexican—American commission. It was not until the 1890s that the commission was actually formed, the two countries surveyed, and the border marked with boundary stones. The United States did not create a Border Patrol agency until 1924, the same year Congress passed sweeping restrictions on Asian and Southern European immigration.[4] In the early days, the Border Patrol was small and underfunded. There were initially 450 agents and they provided their own horses and uniforms. Furthermore, most were stationed at the Canada border, where Asian migrants, the primary target of the legislation, were more likely to cross. Over the years, the mission shifted to patrolling the Mexico border, but as recently as 1990, the Border Patrol was a small force of just over 3,000 agents. Without the resources or infrastructure to close the border completely, the Border Patrol relied on a strategy of interdiction that allowed migrants to cross the border before detaining them on the US side. They were then usually releasing back to Mexico without charges.

In the mid-1990s, in response to criticism of its interdiction methods at the border, the Border Patrol implemented a new deterrence approach that began with "Operation Hold the Line" in El Paso and "Operation Gatekeeper" in San Diego.[5] These two operations fenced critical sections of the border and deployed hundreds of agents to prevent crossings. The operations were hailed as successes because they dramatically reduced the number of crossings to almost zero in the immediate areas of the deployments, which were less than fifteen kilometers (a little over nine miles) long in both cases. Migrants and smugglers simply relocated to another section of the border that was not part of the operation. Nevertheless, the localized success of the operations demonstrated that fences and larger deployments could secure the border.

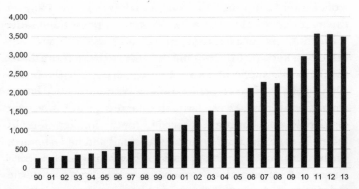

United States Border Patrol budget (in $ millions). Data from United States Border Patrol (cbp.gov/newsroom/media-resources/stats).

The transition to the deterrence model and the subsequent fear of terrorism produced by the September 11, 2001, attacks had three tangible impacts on the US–Mexico border. First, they were used to justify substantial increases in hiring at the Border Patrol. While Operations Gatekeeper and Hold the Line did result in immediate declines in crossings in specific areas, the leadership of the Border Patrol recognized that even with huge increases in funds and personnel, they still would not have enough resources to implement these deterrence tactics on the entire border. Instead, they focused on densely populated and highly trafficked areas, with the goal of discouraging crossings by forcing migrants into remote and dangerous deserts. By 2010 the Border Patrol had more than 20,000 agents. Customs and Border Protection (CBP) employs a total of 59,969 employees, including customs officers, pilots, and maritime interdiction teams.[6] In order to hire such a large number of agents quickly, the Border Patrol removed some previous requirements, such as passing a polygraph exam, and drew heavily on veterans returning from wars in Iraq and Afghanistan, who make up 28.8 percent of agents. The lower standards, combined with the influx of veterans, altered the atmosphere at the agency, bringing a military ethos to the policing job.[7]

Closely related to the funding increases for the Border Patrol is the emergence of a homeland security industry in which military suppliers repurpose weapons, surveillance technologies, and vehicles for use inside the United States. For example, in 2012 the US government spent $18 billion on immigration policing, with the largest amounts for the Border Patrol, Customs, and the Transportation Security Administration—more than the amount spent on all other federal law enforcement combined, including the Federal Bureau of Investigation ($8 billion), the Drug Enforcement Administration ($2.88 billion), the Secret Service ($1 billion), and the Bureau of Alcohol, Tobacco, Firearms and Explosives

($1 billion).[8] Homeland Security Research, an industry analysis firm, estimates that the homeland security industry will be worth an astounding $107.3 billion by 2020.[9] This gives the industry an incentive to lobby Congress substantially to continue to fund border security, regardless of whether it is cost-effective or has any meaningful impact on the number of migrants or the apprehension of terrorists at the border.

The second impact of the increase in funding and attention to the border is the criminalization of migration and a surge in deportations. In the past, most migrants detained at the border were quickly processed and voluntarily repatriated to Mexico, often within a few hours of being caught. This was convenient for the Border Patrol, which had neither the staff necessary to process paperwork nor the space to house thousands of migrants in detention facilities. It was also an acknowledgment that the vast majority of migrants at the border were poor workers, not smugglers or criminals. As the staffing increased and migrant detention facilities were privatized, the government began to detain migrants, charge them with misdemeanors for their first offense and felonies for their second, and then formally deport them. Before 1986 there were rarely more than 20,000 deportations per year; by the mid-2000s, the number was 400,000 per year.[10] The number of migrants in detention facilities increased from 85,000 in 1995 to 440,000 in 2013.[11] Surprisingly, more people have been deported from the United States during the Obama presidency than during any previous administration.[12]

The third change at the border in the aftermath of the September 11 attacks and the adoption of the deterrence philosophy was the construction of substantial border infrastructure that expanded the enforcement area. The new infrastructure includes nine Predator drones—the largest fleet used in US domestic airspace—that patrol the Southwestern border, high-tech surveillance systems known as "smart borders" that use sensors and cameras to monitor for movement at the border,

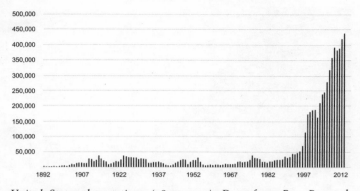

United States deportations (1892–2013). Data from Pew Research Center, US Border Patrol, and Department of Homeland Security Archives (dhs.gov/archives#1).

and ground-penetrating radar designed to detect subterranean tunnels, of which the Border Patrol has found more than 150 since the 1990s.[13] The most visible change in border infrastructure is the construction of the fence at the border. There were no federal fences on the border prior to the short sections built for Operations Hold the Line and Gatekeeper, but today, 1,070 kilometers (670 miles) of the 3,169-kilometer (1,969-mile) border are fenced after the passage of the 2006 Secure Fence Act.[14] The style of fencing varies depending on the terrain and whether it is a vehicle barrier or pedestrian barrier. The pedestrian barrier is 6.4 meters (21 feet) tall and extends 1.8 meters (6 feet) into the ground. It has a metal mesh design that allows wind and light to pass through it, but prevents the passage of objects or humans. While its construction dramatically expanded the amount of fencing at the border, it still leaves two-thirds of the border with Mexico unfenced. During the US presidential nomination period in 2015, Donald Trump and most of the other Republican presidential candidates endorsed building a wall on the remaining section of the border.

United States border fence near El Paso, Texas

From policing to militarized security

The changing practice of border enforcement has led to a blurring of the distinctions between security and policing, on the one hand, and militarization and war-making, on the other.[15] This distinction has historically been a territorial one, with police operating within and up to the state's borderline, while the military exercises its force beyond the territorial extent of the state.[16] Mark Neocleous, professor of government and author of *War Power, Police Power,* suggests that the underlying purposes of the police and the military are the same—to protect the sovereignty of the state from internal and external threats—but the distinction has been maintained to create the perception that internal practices are less severe.[17] Historically, according to justice studies professor Peter Kraska, "the failure of a government to clearly demarcate the two is usually seen as an indicator of repressiveness and lack of democracy."[18]

Despite legal restrictions on military operations in the United States, "the traditional distinctions between military/police, war/law enforcement, and internal/external security are rapidly blurring," a process that accelerated dramatically in the aftermath of the September 11 attacks.[19] The underlying logic of protecting sovereignty is increasingly clear as police and military combine into a single security state.

Border militarization can be most narrowly defined as the deployment of military troops, rather than civilian border patrols, along borders.[20] However, a broader understanding of militarization includes the pervasive influence of military strategies, culture, technologies, hardware, and the combat veterans who are now policing the border. Kraska argues that the proliferation of these "stress[es] the use of force and threat of violence as the most appropriate and efficacious means to solve problems. It emphasizes the exercise of military power, hardware, organization, operations, and technology as its primary problem solving tools."[21] This definition of militarization also includes the application of military ideology in areas outside the traditional roles of the military. "It is the process of arming, organizing, planning, training for, threatening, and sometimes implementing violent conflict."[22]

Police militarization was clearly on display in the aftermath of the shooting of Michael Brown in Ferguson, Missouri, in 2014, when civil rights marchers were met by police in body armor with armored vehicles and assault weapons. Much of this military hardware was obtained by local police departments through the Pentagon's 1033 Program, which since the early 1990s has transferred some $5 billion in excess equipment to civilian law enforcement agencies, including to university police, school districts, and other federal agencies such as Customs and Border Protection. Customs and Border Protection received seventeen cargo planes, ten helicopters, ten bomb robots, and $39 million worth of other security equipment.[23] One irony of this process is that, while the police have been increasingly militarized, the military are increasingly operating in a policing role. The daily activities of US and coalition soldiers in Iraq and Afghanistan have typically included checking documents, raiding houses, and searching for criminals or insurgents in a manner similar to the way SWAT teams conduct drug raids.[24] In May 2015, in the aftermath of the Ferguson protests, President Barack Obama signed an executive order limiting the military gear available to police, but the Border Patrol continues to enjoy access to military hardware. Consequently, the borderline itself is an ideal location to observe how police and military combine into an all-encompassing logic of perpetual war, surveillance, and security.[25]

The Posse Comitatus Act has banned the use of the military within the United States since the nineteenth century. The act was passed after the US Civil War (1861–1865) as part of a series of agreements to remove federal troops from the South during Reconstruction. It reads,

> It shall not be lawful to employ any part of the Army of the United States, as a posse comitatus, or otherwise, for the purpose of executing the laws, except in such cases and under such circumstances as such employment of said force may be expressly authorized by the Constitution or by act of Congress.[26]

In the years after the Civil War, the military colonized what became the western United States. As these wars were won, the US military's focus on external affairs was cemented with the occupation of the Kingdom of Hawai'i, Cuba, Puerto Rico, and the Philippines in the 1890s. Internally, police enforced the law, and the Border Patrol was established in 1924 to monitor the border.[27]

Despite the clear limits on the internal use of the military, Congress has enacted a number of exceptions to the Posse Comitatus Act. These include the National Guard, members of which wear military uniforms but are officially under the authority of the governor of the state in which they are deployed (so-called Title 32 deployments); troops under orders from the president under terms laid out in the 1807 Insurrection Act; troops requested by the Attorney General to protect nuclear materials; those affiliated with the Joint Special Operations Command;[28] missions that support the military's drug interdiction mandate abroad (facilitated through a 1981 change to the law); and training missions.[29] These exceptions have allowed the military a growing role in the internal policing of the border.

In 2006, President George W. Bush's "Operation Jumpstart" mobilized 6,000 National Guard troops at a cost of $1.2 billion. President Barack Obama followed suit in 2010 and 2011 with "Operation Phalanx," which deployed 1,200.[30] Finally, Texas governor Rick Perry requested 1,000 troops for "Operation Strong Safety" in 2014. During Operation Jumpstart, the troops were stationed in specific locations and were allowed neither to move nor to interdict anyone. They could only observe and report what they saw to the Border Patrol. Regardless of the operational success of the missions, each of these deployments played well politically because they demonstrated action by the president in order to deal with a perceived threat at the border. The National Guard troops were under the governor's chain of command, not the Department of Defense's, but that nuance was probably lost on most residents. Deploying it established the perception that deploying the military on the border was both necessary and legal.

Beyond the National Guard, there is already a substantial military presence at the border as part of the so-called War on Drugs and through training missions.[31] The 1989 Defense Authorization Act designated the Department of Defense as the lead agency in tracking and preventing drug smuggling abroad, and it has spent $10 million per year for Title 10 military deployments within the United States in accordance with its drug interdiction mandate.[32] The 204th Military Intelligence Battalion has provided hundreds of hours of support to the Border Patrol, using their sophisticated reconnaissance aircraft to provide live video feeds during Border Patrol operations.[33] The missions are classified as training exercises for the soldiers to practice using the devices, but the applications are real Border Patrol missions.

The most significant military unit that operates at the border is the Joint Task Force–North (JTF–N) based at Fort Bliss in El Paso, Texas, which helps build roads along the border, provides communications and logistics support, and participates in joint operations with the Border Patrol in a support role. JTF–N has been at the forefront of converting military technologies developed in wars in Iraq and Afghanistan to domestic uses. An Army press release from 2012 about "Operation Big Miguel" explained, "Technology originally created for use in tracking improvised explosive device networks in Afghanistan and Iraq is finding new purpose in supporting U.S. Customs and Border Protection by providing mission overwatch during border patrol missions."[34] The connection between wars abroad and the militarization of the border is made explicit here. Not only are the troops on the border using their battlefield experience, they are also bringing along battlefield technologies. Later in the press release, the commander states that he personally put the Border Patrol in touch with the appropriate military contractors so they could order the new hardware.[35] In 2013, JTF–N deployed part of a Stryker armored vehicle brigade, one of the most sophisticated vehicles the military possess.[36] The CBP's drone fleet is also an example of this transformation.

Placing uniformed military troops on the border has a powerful symbolic and normative effect. It also contributes to media narratives that describe the border as a war zone. For example, for several years, Fox News labeled stories about the US–Mexico border with the title "America's Third War," implying that the situation at the border was equivalent to the US wars in Iraq and Afghanistan. Similarly, television shows like the National Geographic channel's *Border Wars*, which aired for five seasons between 2010 and 2013, depicted the border as a war zone where agents were fighting a constant battle against drug cartels and terrorists. The changes in the practice of the Border Patrol, the use of the military at the border, and the depiction of the border in the media as a violent and dangerous place contribute to the structural violence of the Mexican border as the line on a map from the 1840s has become a militarized zone to prevent the movement of migrants.

Death at the border

The militarization and securitization of the border has resulted in far too many stories similar to that of Sergio Guereca's killing. From 2010 to 2015, US Border Patrol agents shot and killed thirty-three people.[37] These killings became an issue in the summer of 2014 with the firing of internal affairs chief James Tomsheck. The Border Patrol stated that it fired Tomsheck for not investigating killings, but Tomsheck alleged his firing was part of a cover-up to prevent him from investigating. In an interview with National Public Radio, Tomsheck stated that he believed that 25 percent of the fatal shootings were suspicious: "Some persons in leadership positions in the Border Patrol were either fabricating or distorting information to give the outward appearance that it was an appropriate use of lethal force when in fact it was not."[38] Similarly, a 2014 report by the American Immigration Council found that of 809 reports of abuse between 2009 and 2012—and reports are very rare due to the subordinate position of many migrants—in 97 percent of the cases no action was taken.[39] In media interviews, Tomsheck said that the problem is the culture of the Border Patrol, whose agents think of themselves as part of the military. "The phrase was frequently used—a 'paramilitary border security force' or a 'paramilitary homeland security force,'" said Tomsheck.[40]

In response to criticism, the Border Patrol issued revised guidelines in May 2014 that state that agents can use deadly force when there is a "reasonable belief that the subject of such force poses an imminent danger of death or serious physical injury to the officer/agent or to another person."[41] Consequently, agents can still use force against people throwing rocks when the agent perceives the threat of death or grave injury. In April 2015, the Fifth District US Court of Appeals ruled against a civil suit by Sergio Guereca's parents because "a Mexican citizen standing in Mexico" has no standing in a US court. The Guereca family attorney, Marion Reilly, summed up the ruling: "So the court has ruled that it was appropriate for the agent to kill an unarmed teenager based on his nationality—don't kill him if he is a US citizen, but fire away if he is a Mexican."[42]

The US–Mexico border is also characterized by violence on the Mexican side as cartels work to solidify control over profitable smuggling routes. Such routes exist only because the border creates regulatory differences on either side, with drugs and people moving into the United States and weapons moving into Mexico. The US government estimates that wholesale drug profits to Colombian and Mexican cartels are between $18 and $39 billion annually, despite—or perhaps because of—the hardening of the border and the decades-long drug war in the US.[43] Some of the worst violence struck Ciudad Juárez from 2008 to 2012 as the Juárez cartel and the Sinaloa cartel fought for control of the city. This resulted in 1,600 murders in 2008, 2,600 in 2009, and more than 3,000 in 2010. Migrants from other parts of Central and South America are often targets for extortion and kidnapping near the border and on their way north through Mexico. In a

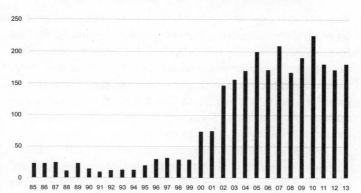

Migrant deaths in the Tucson, Arizona, sector of the United States border. Data from B. Anderson and B. Parks, "Symposium on Border Crossing Deaths: Introduction," Journal of Forensic Sciences, 53, 2008, 6–7, and Brian and Laczko, Fatal Journeys.

six-month period in 2010, 11,000 migrants were reported to have been kidnapped in Mexico.[44] Between 2007 and 2013, an estimated 47,000 migrants died in Mexico. Many were killed by gangs, but others fell off trains, died in car crashes, or succumbed to the elements before reaching the border.[45] Despite the dangers of the journey, thousands of people continue to flee their home countries due to deteriorating conditions there.

Unfortunately, direct violence, including killings by the Border Patrol, does not even scratch the surface of the structural violence that surrounds the US–Mexico border. The Border Patrol has recovered more than 6,000 bodies along the US–Mexico border since the 1990s, deaths attributable to the construction of the border wall and the massive Border Patrol presence. Migrants are funneled to more dangerous and remote locations, just like migrants at the edges of the EU. Instead of crossing in a city, migrants are making the arduous journey through the deserts of Arizona, which requires hiking for fifty or more kilometers through arid and desolate terrain.[46] According to the first National Border

Patrol Strategy document, released in 1994, that was the goal: "The prediction is that with traditional entry and smuggling routes disrupted, illegal traffic will be deterred, or forced over more hostile terrain, less suited for crossing and more suited for enforcement."[47] Put another way, the official Border Patrol strategy was to create conditions that would cause more migrants to die in hostile terrain, in order to deter other migrants from making the trip.

The data demonstrate that this new Border Patrol strategy worked very quickly. With the increased enforcement, crossings and migrant deaths in California declined, while those in Arizona surged. The Tucson, Arizona, coroner's office has seen a twentyfold increase in the number of migrant bodies found per year since the 1990s.[48] Migrants do not bring enough food and water, often because smugglers, who do not want to be slowed down by the extra weight, tell them the trip is not very far. The harrowing result is documented in books such as *The Devil's Highway* by Luís Alberto Urrea, which tells the story of twenty-six migrants who attempted to enter the United States through the Arizona desert in May 2001.[49] Only twelve survived. Leanne Weber and Sharon Pickering of the Monash University criminal justice program estimate that there are two additional deaths for every recovered body, citing the harsh conditions in the vast and remote deserts, where remains are quickly obscured by shifting sands.[50]

The militarization of the US–Mexico border symbolizes a global trend toward hardened and securitized borders. In the era of globalization, as the gap between the wealthiest and poorest states has grown, states around the world have deployed new security infrastructure along borders, designed to detect and prevent the movement of the world's poor. The militarization of borders today is not directed toward an existential threat to the sovereignty of the state, such as an invasion by a neighboring army. Instead, the full force of modern military technology is oriented toward smugglers profiting from different regulations on either side of the border and migrant workers looking for better opportunities. The US Border Patrol operates as if it is part of the military; the actual US military plays a significant role in internal policing at the border. The historic distinction between the internal and external roles of the police and military has blurred, and the border is a key site where the emerging security state is visible and where privileges are maintained by restricting movement through violence.

Chapter 3

The Global Border Regime

The European Union's and United States' border security policies have become normalized, and constructing barriers to prevent so-called illegal crossings is now seen as a key function of the state. But these wealthy Western states are not the only ones restricting movement at borders through walls, security agents, and mutual agreements with neighboring states. Instead, states as diverse as Israel, India, Bangladesh, and Australia are engaging in similar practices, with similarly devastating consequences for people who want to move.

The Abu Rahma family

There is little to suggest why Bil'in became the epicenter of the grassroots Palestinian movement against the construction of the Israeli wall in the West Bank. Bil'in is a tiny hamlet perched on a ridge, with a population of only 1,700. The landscape of low-slung homes, dusty roads, and olive trees clinging to rugged hillsides is no different than dozens of other Palestinian towns throughout the West Bank. Just like in many other towns, the wall cuts straight through Bil'in's land, uprooting olive trees and cutting the villagers off from their fields on the lower slopes and in the valley below. Bil'in is adjacent to the Israeli settlement of Modi'in Illit, which has a circular shape and tightly packed high-rise apartments that evoke the walled cities of medieval Europe.

In order to get a better sense of how the construction of the wall affects the town, I visited Bil'in and met with Mohammed Khatib, the head of the Bil'in council. He explained to me that while many towns were devastated by the route of the wall, the people of Bil'in were particularly steadfast in their refusal to accept the occupation of their lands. He pointed to the media-savvy leadership of the village. "It started at the local level," he told me when I visited his house in July 2010, "but now it is more. It is a national symbol of the national struggle. Also, now we have learned how to make it an international struggle." Since 2005, every Friday after the noon prayers there are protests against the wall and the occupation that attract dozens to a few hundred Palestinian and international activists. The protests in Bil'in start peacefully, but almost always end with the Israel Defense Forces (IDF) firing tear gas to disperse the crowd.

After we finished talking, Mohammed directed me to the home of the Abu Rahmas, a family that has experienced the violence of borders to an extent that is hard to imagine. We sat in the living room of their home, which included a few brown chairs, a bed, and a wooden table. Like the streets of Palestinian cities and the homes of many Palestinian families, the Abu Rahmas' living-room walls were adorned with posters that paid tribute to acts of resistance against the Israeli occupation. The difference was that the posters in their house depicted family members as revolutionaries and martyrs to the cause. Two Abu Rahma children have been killed near the border fence, and two more have been arrested by the IDF. While we talked, Jawaher, their thirty-six-year-old daughter, handed me a tear-gas canister shot by the Israelis during one of the weekly protests against the wall. It was black with a rubbery slick surface and a few scratches on the sides, hard and heavy but small, the size of a medium potato.

Until April 2009, Ashraf, who was twenty-nine at the time of my visit, was the most well-known member of the family. Ashraf, who is shy and awkward but also fearless, is a famous revolutionary whose protests against the occupation, which have led to multiple arrests and worse, are regularly featured on the news. His olive skin and scruffy facial hair evoke Che Guevara, the iconic communist revolutionary, and many of the posters include images of Guevara as well. Ashraf showed me videos of two of his escapades, one ending in triumph, the other in agony.[1] On May 26, 2008, Ashraf and several other Palestinian activists snuck into the Modi'in Illit construction site, which is on their village's land, and attempted to stop the work. Ashraf scaled the boom of an enormous construction crane and unfurled a Palestinian flag. The video shows him surprisingly high up the steep boom, with befuddled construction workers and Israeli settlers milling around the base. The IDF eventually arrived; after five hours they were able to lower the boom of the crane. They arrested Ashraf and took him to prison, where he was held for a week. A month after his release, on July 7, 2008, Ashraf went to Nil'in, another village along the route of the wall where there are protests against the occupation, to deliver supplies. The village was under a four-day curfew and Ashraf was stopped at a checkpoint. Reporters were barred from entering Nil'in at the time, but the video of the encounter was taken by a seventeen-year-old girl, Salaam Kanan, who lived near the checkpoint and had been trying to document what was going on. In the video, Ashraf stands blindfolded with his hands tied behind his back beside the sandy barricades and barbed wire. An IDF vehicle and a number of soldiers, guns raised, are on the far side. Ashraf looks small and vulnerable in the face of the security apparatus that has engulfed him. Seconds later, one of the soldiers shoots him in the leg. He crumples to the ground. Luckily, the bullet hit his thick boots, which resulted in only a minor injury.[2] As we finished watching the video, Ashraf's mother, Subhiya, jumped into the conversation: "He did not even tell us what happened to him in Nil'in. We saw it later on television. He disappeared for three days and did not tell us about it when he returned."

As Ashraf recounted both stories, he maintained a mischievous grin. "Why should I be afraid?" he asked. "They already shot me in Nil'in. What else can they do?"

The Abu Rahmas' protests against the Israeli wall took a tragic turn on April 17, 2009, a sunny day with a few wispy white clouds.[3] The protests began after Friday prayers, as local families and international activists gathered and marched the few hundred meters down to the wall, where the IDF soldiers were already waiting for them. The protestors chanted slogans and carried signs and flags. Ashraf's brother Bassem frequently flew a kite along the border fence, its simplicity contrasting with the weapons, walls, and body armor of the Israelis. The Palestinians describe their protests as peaceful; they do not carry guns or knives. However, after a few minutes, they often begin throwing rocks at the Israeli soldiers. The soldiers wait patiently for this provocation and then respond with overwhelming force, dispersing the crowd with tear gas and detaining the protestors they say threw rocks. The discontinuity of power at borders is evident here, just as it was in killing of Sergio Guereca, discussed in chapter 2. The external threat is very low—people throwing rocks—but the response nevertheless employs the full force of a modern military. In 2015, Israeli prime minister Benjamin Netanyahu announced a new emphasis on rock-throwing, with the possibility of "changing the protocol for open-fire orders on rock throwers, establishing a minimum sentence for rock throwers, and levying a heavy fine on minors throwing rocks and their families." Netanyahu explained, "We are declaring war on those who throw stones and bottles, and rioters."[4]

In videos of the protests on that fateful April day, twenty-nine-year-old Bassem is easy to spot, in jeans and a fluorescent yellow soccer jersey: Fiat #11. He is stockier than Ashraf and has a clean-shaven face and shorter, neater hair. He walks with the procession, then yells across at the Israeli soldiers that they are on the occupied land of the village. The soldiers issue warnings via megaphone that it is a military area and the protestors should disperse. Bassem yells back that they are on occupied land. A few protestors carrying Palestinian flags and shields walk past Bassem toward the Israelis' position. No one throws rocks today, but the protestors with the flags are so close to the fence that the provocation is apparently enough. A buzzer goes off on the Israeli side, signaling for the soldiers to take action to disperse the crowd. They fire some tear-gas canisters, there are screams, and some of the protestors turn back at the sound of shots. The camera pans around, following their retreat, then turns back to the Israelis. The protestors with the flags and shield continue to move slowly toward the fence and the Israeli position. More tear gas. More yelling. Bassem is beside the cameraperson, behind a second waist-high fence, but within three or four meters (ten or twelve feet) of the action. He and the camera operator do not have shields.

It is a windy day, which makes the tear gas less effective. It blows away and the protestors move upwind. More canisters, more yelling. A few soldiers leave their fortified position and move up to the fence. They are only a yard from the protestors, with the flags and shields. Uncomfortably close. Bassem is yelling for the Israelis to go away. Then there is the whiz of a tear-gas canister. Bassem's yelling becomes an agonized scream. The camera pans around and down to Bassem writhing on the ground, with his hands on his chest and the first signs of blood oozing between his fingers. The whole tragedy took less than two minutes.

Bassem's mother was at the house when she got word that something had happened to Bassem. "I started wailing, even though I did not know at that point that he was dead," she explained to me. "When I saw my other sons were crying, then I knew."

I look at the tear-gas canister in my hands. "Is this the actual canister?" I ask. The family nods. I'm not sure what to do, so I take a picture of Ashraf holding it. He grins.

© Reece Jones 2016

Ashraf Abu Rahma and the tear gas canister

Israel has the most complete border fencing and security network in the world. The best-known Israeli wall is the barrier in the West Bank, which was begun in 2002. The planned route of 620 kilometers (385 miles) is approximately two-thirds complete. The West Bank wall is controversial because it does not follow the boundaries of the state of Israel that are codified at the United Nations. Instead, more than 80 percent of the route is built in the West Bank, on land that Israel occupied after the 1967 Six-Day War. The wall is condemned by human rights groups like the Israeli organization B'tselem; in 2004 the International Court of Justice, an arm of the UN that provides nonbinding advisory opinions to the UN General Assembly, called it contrary to international law. Most of the Israeli barrier consists of three layers of barbed-wire fencing, with roads and surveillance systems along the entire route. The imposing concrete wall—a more readily recognizable symbol, at eight meters (twenty-six feet) tall double the height of the Berlin Wall—only accounts for about 5 percent of the route in the major cities of Bethlehem, Jerusalem, Ramallah, Qalqilyah, and Tulkarm. Israel also built a fence on its border with Lebanon after its withdrawal from southern Lebanon in 2000. Its border with Syria, in the occupied Golan Heights, is fenced, as are its borders with Gaza (following the 2005 with-drawal), Egypt (since 2011, to keep out African migrants and armed militant groups from the Sinai Peninsula), and Jordan (since 2014).[5] Israel is literally a fortress state, with walls and security infrastructure on all of its land borders.

Israel's poor diplomatic relations with its neighboring countries play a role, but the underlying purpose of its border work is to establish its authority and clearly demarcate where its sovereignty begins and its neighboring states end. While the United States expanded its territory in the mid-1800s and has worked to incorporate the new lands into the American mythology for a century and a half, Israel is still in the process of defining its territorial extent. The wall is only part of this process, which also includes the construction of Israeli settle-ments in the West Bank, the use of Israeli-only highways, the recognition of historic sites in the West Bank such as Rachel's Tomb in Bethlehem as Jewish heritage sites, and the reclassi-fication of much of the land as nature reserves to prevent the construction of Palestinian homes. The result of these prac-tices over the past forty years is that large sections of the land in the West Bank have been transformed from Palestinian-Arab space into Israeli space.[6]

The Israeli government is pulled in multiple directions in this process. Israel is a UN member state and is obligated to respect the territorial integrity and sovereignty of other member states, like Egypt, Jordan, Lebanon, and Syria. Palestine has not yet become a full UN member, so its territory is not for-mally established, although it is recognized bilaterally by 136 UN member states. Within Israel, powerful organizations such as the Jewish Home party argue that biblical Israel included all of the land from the Mediterranean to the Jordan River—all of contemporary Israel and Palestine—and that the state of Israel should work to control that land. The settler movement in Israel works by this logic and the government has encour-aged the resettlement of hundreds of thousands of Israelis into these lands. A political agreement between Israel and Palestine is elusive because the older Green Line—the boundary of the West Bank from 1948 to 1967 and the official border of Israel at the UN—no longer matches the settlement patterns of Israelis on the ground. If one includes the lands that Israel has annexed around Jerusalem, approximately 400,000 Israeli citizens live in the West Bank. If the Green Line became the official border of Palestine, there would be hundreds of thousands of Israelis in the Palestinian state. If the border was moved to incorporate more of the West Bank into Israel, there would be hundreds of thousands of Palestinians in Israel, signifying a further erosion of Palestinian control.

The Israeli walls in the West Bank are an offensive strategy to solidify claims to more territory, not a defensive barrier to protect already existing Israeli space. They affect the movement of Palestinians and sever Palestinians' connection to the city of Jerusalem. The Israeli settlements form a loop around the outside of the city, making it difficult for Palestinians to travel between other parts of Palestine and East Jerusalem. These difficulties are compounded by unpredictable checkpoints that can add hours of unexpected delays to any journey. The wall typically runs between Israeli settlements such as Modi'in Illit and nearby Palestinian towns such as Bil'in, but places all of the farmland in between on the Israeli side. The wall cuts through farms and pastures, its construction uprooting thousands of olive trees that had dotted the landscape for centuries. Palestinians are cut off from their farms and cannot support themselves.

Khatib explained the psychological impact of the occupation and the wall, which combine to limit where people can build and prevent them from working. After residents began to protest the construction of the wall on their lands, the IDF began to target them for arrest and interrogation. The worst, however, were the night raids, which were a collective punishment designed to frighten the entire population. "Take my son, for example. They came here one night with their faces painted to arrest me," Khatib explained, detailing his arrest on January 28, 2010, when the IDF stormed his house at 1:45 A.M. and held his wife and four kids at gunpoint for several hours.[7] "My son, he is afraid to go to his bedroom now because of it. Now every time he sees a soldier he is scared."

In October 2011, a few months after my visit with the Abu Rahma family, Ashraf was arrested by the IDF for allegedly throwing stones during a demonstration and was taken to Ofer Prison, an Israeli facility in the West Bank that holds approximately 1,100 Palestinian prisoners. In early 2016, he was still being held. Two months after Ashraf's arrest, in December 2011, tragedy struck the Abu Rahma family again. Jawaher Abu Rahma died after choking on fumes from another tear gas canister fired near their home, which is only a few hundred meters from the protest site.[8] The Israeli authorities deny responsibility for the deaths of both Bassem and Jawaher. In 2013, investigators closed the case on Bassem's death, citing a lack of evidence. In Jawaher's case, the IDF suggested that she might not have been near the protests and that medical records were inconclusive on the cause of death.[9]

Felani

While the borders of the European Union and the United States have resulted in tens of thousands of deaths in the past decade as migrants are funneled to more dangerous crossing points, the India–Bangladesh border has the highest number of deaths at the hands of a state security service, India's Border Security Force (BSF). From 2000 to 2015, the BSF killed more than a thousand Bangladeshi civilians along the border.[10] One of the most troubling accounts is the story of fifteen-year-old Felani Khatun, whose killing made the international news.[11] Felani and her family were undocumented Bangladeshi migrants living in New Delhi, India. Her father, Nurul Islam, had gone there when he was six years old; Felani was born there. By some estimates, there are 15 million Bangladeshi migrants living in India. Most of them are in West Bengal, where their native Bengali language is spoken and the culture is similar to that of Bangladesh. Others, like the Khatun family, choose to live in Delhi, the densely packed Indian capital, where they blend in with millions of other slum dwellers. Migrants are stigmatized and blamed for crime in India, but the better job opportunities and wages make the difficult life worth it for many.

Nurul and Felani were traveling back to Bangladesh to begin the process of looking for a husband for Felani in January 2011. Although, officially, all Bangladeshis need a visa to visit India, the vast majority of people continue to cross the border without documents. Getting a passport is an arduous and expensive task and is often beyond the means of many of the poor of Bangladesh. Furthermore, India would deny the visas of most poor laborers, which would prevent them from traveling legally anyway. Nurul and Felani arrived at the Indian side of the border and paid a smuggler 3,000 rupees, or roughly $50, to arrange for their crossing of the border. Many people cross by boat along one of the many unfenced rivers that meander back and forth across the border. However, Felani and her dad were given a ladder and instructed to climb over the border fence in the early morning fog.

The border between India and Bangladesh is a relic of the 1947 partition of British India. When the British left India, different options were weighed for organizing the newly independent state. One was to leave behind a united India that would have included all of the former British lands, an idea that still has traction in some parts of South Asia today. Another was to create a dozen new states based on language groups, whose land area and population would be similar to many European states (Bengali, Gujarati, Hindi, Marathi,

Punjabi, Tamil, Telugu, and Urdu all have over 50 million native speakers today). Nevertheless, in consultation with Jawaharlal Nehru, the leader of the Indian Congress Party, and Muhammad Jinnah, the leader of the Muslim League, the British decided to partition India based on religion by linking together the two areas with majority Muslim populations as a single state of Pakistan. This divided both the Punjabi and Bengali language communities and set off the movement of 14 million people in the following weeks, as families who found themselves on the wrong side of the border moved to where their religion was in the majority. This movement of Hindus to India and Muslims to Pakistan represented the largest mass migration in history. An estimated million people were killed in the violent aftermath. In the decades since, India and Pakistan have gone to war four times and continue to disagree over the territory of Kashmir, a Muslim-majority princely state whose leader nevertheless chose to join India after the partition.

The trauma of Partition did not end until the early 1970s for residents of what is today Bangladesh. After the dust settled, the Muslim residents of South Asia found themselves in the unwieldy state of Pakistan. The two halves of Pakistan—what are today Pakistan and Bangladesh—were 1,500 kilometers apart and lacked a common language. They also had no historical political connections. Unsurprisingly, the two halves began to pull apart within a few years, as military dictatorships based in West Pakistan restricted the political power of East Pakistan (today's Bangladesh). An independence movement began in Bangladesh, based on the rallying cry that the people of Bengal had a separate culture, language, and heritage that deserved an independent state.[12] The movement culminated with a 1971 civil war and the recognition of Bangladesh as an independent state in the early 1970s. Bangladesh joined the UN in 1974.

Bangladesh literally means "the country of the Bengalis," but its independence created an odd situation in which more than a third of all Bengali speakers live across the border in India, in the state of West Bengal. Furthermore, Kolkata, the cultural, economic, and political heart of Bengal for centuries, is located outside the country of the Bengalis, which is something akin to Paris not being in France. Nevertheless, the passage of time, the post-Partition migrations, and nation-making practices on both sides have allowed the two places to become differentiated. Bangladeshi citizens were united in the afterglow of a successful independence movement, while residents of West Bengal became integrated into an Indian state that was oriented toward Delhi and in which English and Hindi were the more commonly used national languages.[13]

Prior to 2000, the India–Bangladesh border was open and lightly guarded. For many decades after the 1947 partition, local residents continued to cross the border, which was little more than a line on a map, not a real border on the ground. People from both sides would visit relatives and friends across the border, go to the market in the other country, or even help neighbors on the other side of the line harvest their crops. However, in the six decades since Partition, the neighboring countries have slowly and unevenly marked the boundary and tried to enforce it.[14] In the 1950s, border stones were laid to mark the line on the ground. In the 1960s, border security forces were created; they primarily worked at crossing points, processing documents and conducting customs inspections. In the 1980s, India began building some fencing on the border between Bangladesh and the Indian state of Assam, where there was discontent over migration from Bangladesh. Nevertheless, most of the border remained open until the early 2000s, when the Indian government began to focus on the threat of terrorism. The most notorious attack in India was the siege in Mumbai, in which a band of terrorists from Pakistan killed 164 people over several days, but India had a major attack every year from 2000 to 2010. As part of the effort to confront this threat, the government worked to gain control over its borders, ostensibly to prevent the entry of terrorists but also to stem the flow of migrants from Bangladesh. In 2015, India's home minister, Rajnath Singh, reiterated that the government planned to "completely seal" the border. "We want to take all possible steps to check illegal immigration. All loopholes have to be plugged."[15]

While Israel has the world's most complete system of border walls, India has the most kilometers of fences and walls: 1,926 kilometers (1,198 miles) of its 2,308-kilometer (1,434-mile) border with Pakistan, as well as sections of its 1,624-kilometer (1,009 km) border with Myanmar. India also has the largest border security force in the world, with more than 200,000 agents. At the Bangladesh border, the changes of the past decade meant increases in the number of Border Security Force agents—who were usually from another part of India and did not speak Bengali—and the construction of over 3,500 kilometers (2,175 miles) of fence along the 4,090-kilometer (2,541-mile) border. The agents are the front line against terrorism in India and have standing orders to shoot to kill if they perceive a terrorist infiltration threat.[16]

Felani and her father Nurul arrived at this newly securitized and militarized border at 8:30 on the foggy morning of January 7, 2011. The landscape of the border is surprisingly beautiful, with palm trees and bright green rice paddies planted right up to the edge of the fence. Felani and her father brought a small bamboo ladder provided by the smugglers and propped it up on the Indian side. Nurul easily climbed over the fence, then instructed his daughter to climb. Felani wore a shalwar kameez, the traditional attire of unmarried women in South Asia. Hers was bright red, white, and blue, with long, flowing edges that stretched down past her knees. Felani made it up the ladder, but her clothing became entangled in the barbed wire at the top. She started to scream, which alerted the border guards to their location in the fog. Following his shoot-to-kill orders, Amiya Ghosh, an Indian

BSF constable, shot at what he perceived to be an unauthorized infiltration into India.

Felani Khatun's body dangled on the barbed-wire fence for several hours after she was shot. She was alive for a while and asked for water. The sun burned off the fog and by late morning her body, in the brightly colored shalwar kameez, was visible from a distance. Crowds gathered. When the BSF finally took her down, they did not place her on a gurney or in a body bag. Instead, they tied her feet and arms to a bamboo pole and carried her back to India like an animal. The photos of her body hanging on the fence and then on the bamboo pole produced outrage in Bangladesh and around the world.

Although there was little doubt that the killing was within the BSF's shoot-to-kill rules, in order to quell the international criticism, the government of India convened a special court, reserved for military and security force investigations, to rule on the matter. After deliberating, the five-man court acquitted the constable, who apparently admitted to the shooting, because the evidence was "inconclusive and insufficient." Felani's family and their lawyer, Abraham Lincoln—in Bangladesh it is not uncommon for parents to be explicit with their hopes when naming their children—were outraged. Lincoln said, "It can encourage the BSF's mindless attitude, giving the killings legality."[17] Although the trial ended in an acquittal, it was significant that there was a trial: it is the only time a BSF constable has been prosecuted for a shooting at the border. None of the other thousand Bangladeshi citizens shot and killed by the Indian Border Security Force between 2000 and 2015 even got that much.

The Rohingya

Bangladesh is almost completely surrounded by India, but it does have a short 200-kilometer (125-mile) border with

Myanmar (Burma), which is the locus of another migration crisis. The difference is that on this border, Bangladesh is the country patrolling for migrants and trying to prevent unauthorized movements. The border between Bangladesh and Myanmar is another relic of British colonization that failed to consider local population dynamics.

The Rohingya are a Muslim minority population of approximately 1.1 million people who live in Rakhine State in the northwestern corner of Myanmar. Myanmar is a predominantly Buddhist country, with 90 percent of the population following that faith. The government has long contended that the Rohingya are not natives of Myanmar but immigrants who crossed over from Bangladesh. Consequently, they are not given citizenship and are persecuted in Myanmar.[18] In 1982 the government of Burma—it did not change its name to Myanmar until 1989—passed a restrictive citizenship law that limited citizenship to specific ethnic groups (Kachin, Kayah, Karen, Chin, Burman, Mon, Rakhine, Shan, Kaman, and Zerbadee) or people who could prove their ancestors had resided within the borders of the country before 1823, which marked the arrival of the British. Rohingya was not included in the accepted ethnic groups and it was almost impossible for most to document residence before 1823, which means that the Rohingya are stateless people without the rights of citizenship in Myanmar.[19]

For its part, Bangladesh denies that the Rohingya originated there and only provides basic services in refugee camps for Rohingya who cross the border. The migration began twenty years ago. Today more than 200,000 people live in mud huts in the camps along the Naf River, which separates Bangladesh and Myanmar. Bangladesh lacks the resources to adequately deal with the refugees and wants them to return to Myanmar. "The Rohingya are the citizens of Myanmar and they must go back," H. T. Imam, a Bangladesh official, explained in 2015 to a Reuters reporter. "We feel for them, but we are unable to host them any longer."[20]

As a stateless people in Myanmar, the Rohingya are denied access to many rights and protections. As foreigners, according to the government, they have to get special permits to travel within Myanmar or to go abroad. Many are forced to labor for the military and provide them with food and supplies.[21] In 2012, Buddhist activist groups attacked Muslims and Muslim-owned businesses across Myanmar as they tried to protect the Buddhist culture of the country from what they perceived to be an attempt to impose Islam. Ashin Wirathu, a Buddhist monk who was jailed from 2003 to 2012 for inciting religious violence, is the spiritual leader of the movement and has openly referred to Muslims as enemies and dogs, calling for boycotts of Muslim businesses and providing the ideology that is the foundation for attacks on Muslims across Myanmar. A 2015 study produced by the Allard K. Lowenstein International Human Rights Clinic at Yale Law School found "persuasive evidence that the crime of genocide had been committed against Rohingya Muslims."[22]

As the government of Bangladesh is less welcoming and the border is fenced and patrolled against migrations, the Rohingya have begun to look for stability elsewhere. The United Nations High Commissioner for Refugees estimates that 25,000 Rohingya departed in boats from the Myanmar–Bangladesh border area in the first four months of 2015.[23] After weeks on the crowded and dirty boats, they were not met with the welcome they were hoping for. Several boats were reportedly pushed away from the coasts of Indonesia, Malaysia, and Thailand before Indonesia and Malaysia, under growing international pressure, eventually took them. Thailand continues to refuse to accept any of the refugees. The deputy home minister of Malaysia, Wan Junaidi, explained the position of the receiving countries: "What do you expect us to do? We have been very nice to the people who broke into our border. We have treated them humanely, but they cannot be flooding our shores like this. We have to send the right message that they are not welcome here," he told the Associated Press.[24]

In addition to the hundreds of people who have died en route, in August 2015 Malaysia discovered several mass graves near its border with Thailand that were reported to be of Rohingya migrants who died or were killed by smugglers. The focus on the misdeeds of smugglers is similar to the response to the Mediterranean migration issue: shifting the blame away from the restrictive policies of the receiving states and onto unscrupulous human traffickers. For the Rohingya, the ambiguity of their origins has allowed some government officials in Indonesia and Australia to suggest that many are not refugees at all. Because the Rohingya are stateless and cannot demonstrate where they come from, it is easier for governments uncomfortable with taking refugees to deny them the protection of refugee status. Australian foreign affairs minister Julie Bishop said most were Bangladeshi "illegal laborers," siding with the exclusionary views of the Myanmar government.[25]

Australia

For many migrants hoping to reach Australia, the trip begins with a comfortable airplane journey to Jakarta, Indonesia. Iranian and Iraqi citizens do not need a visa to visit Indonesia, so many migrants save or borrow money to buy a plane ticket first before meeting with smugglers in Indonesia, who assist them in their journey by boat to Australia. Despite the upscale start to their journey, once they are in Indonesia, the migrants endure similar hardships to those of migrants attempting to enter the European Union by boat. They are ferried around in the backs of pickup trucks and housed in crowded conditions in dilapidated buildings in the capital and port towns along the coast of Java.[26] Australia has extremely strict border policies that do not allow boats to reach Australia, which prevents easier crossings from the Indonesian island of Timor, across the Timor Sea, to the mainland of Australia. Instead, most migrants attempt the more dangerous and distant journey from Java across the open Indian Ocean toward Christmas Island, an Australia territory 400 kilometers (250 miles) away.

Christmas Island was discovered on Christmas Day 1643 by an English ship. Today it supports approximately 2,000 full-time residents. The island was a British colony for centuries until the Australian government bought it in 1959. Its primary value lies in its phosphorus mines. Most of the tiny island (135 square kilometers, or 52 square miles—about 1.5 times the size of Manhattan) is a nature reserve, because its isolated location has allowed for the evolution of many unique and endemic species of fauna and flora.

Migrants began to arrive in the early 1990s. In response, the Australian government reclassified the island as outside Australian territory for immigration purposes, which means that migrants cannot automatically apply for asylum in Australia. Instead they are placed in a migration detention

Australian migration poster. Australian Government Department of Immigration and Border Protection.

facility, which often houses more people than the entire population of the island. Christmas Island has also seen tragedies similar to those that have occurred in the Mediterranean. In December 2010, a boat was smashed on the rocks of the island, killing forty-eight migrants. In total, the Australian Border Deaths Database counts 1,974 deaths of migrants between January 2000 and November 2015.[27]

Australia attempts to deter migrants with posters and advertisements that emphasize the dangers of the journey. One poster campaign states in big bold red letters: "NO WAY: you will not make Australia home" with an image of a small ship tossed in giant waves in the background. The campaign includes translations of the warnings in Albanian, Arabic, Bahasa Indonesia, Bengali, Dari, Farsi, Hindi, Kurdish Sorani, Nepalese, Pashto, Rohingya, Sinhala, Somali, Sudanese Arabic, Tamil, Urdu, and Vietnamese.[28]

Migrants who attempt the trip are often detained at sea before they reach Australia. The government of Australia has agreements to house these migrants in detention facilities in other countries, including East Timor and Nauru, which means they never actually set foot on Australian soil while their claims are adjudicated. The conditions in some of the Australian detention facilities are atrocious, and long delays in the claim process mean that some migrants are stuck there for years at a time.[29] The facility in Nauru is particularly bleak. Nauru is a tiny South Pacific island state, one-seventh the size of Christmas Island, with a population of fewer than 10,000 people. After the phosphorus that drove the country's economy was exhausted, the government welcomed aid from Australia in exchange for hosting the migrants. Conditions in the facility are obscured because Nauru does not grant visas to journalists; however, government reports point to violence, unsanitary conditions, and long delays that break the will of many migrants. "This detention is created in such a way as to act as a deterrent, to encourage people to return [to their homeland], and to stop other people trying to seek asylum," Peter Young, a doctor who worked in the facilities, told the *Guardian*. "The harmfulness is a 'designed-in' feature."[30]

The global picture

These examples of perilous border crossings could go on and on. Movement is a problem for all states in the global system. Most states enforce their borders through violence that often results in deaths, and the people who are killed at borders are rarely militants or terrorists. Many are kids, like Sergio Guereca, Felani Khatun, and Aylan Kurdi, or people like Bassem and Jawaher Abu Rahma, whose lives were turned upside down and then ended by the construction of a border near their home. Others are smugglers using the different regulations on either side of the border to make some money, refugees fleeing war, or poor people looking for a better life.

Contrary to the arguments of a number of scholars and commentators that globalization is undermining the position of the state, the global scale of border violence demonstrates that the state remains the dominant container of political power in the world.[31] Thomas Friedman, the *New York Times* columnist, suggested that "the world is flat" because the Internet and communication technologies are connecting people around the world, giving them equal access to the global economy. More recently, Wendy Brown, political science professor at the University of California at Berkeley and author of *Walled States, Waning Sovereignty,* has argued that border walls and militarized security efforts are not a sign of strength but the last gasps of a dying political system based on territorially defined nation-states.[32] Brown writes, "Counterintuitively, perhaps, it is the weakening of state sovereignty, and more precisely, the detachment of sovereignty from the nation-state, that is generating much of the frenzy of nation-state wall building today."[33] As a result of states' perceived waning of authority over what happens within their borders, scholars in this camp see new walls as a losing attempt to reassert some claim to sovereign authority over decisions in that space.

There is little doubt that the changes Friedman and Brown identify represent a reorientation of the role of the state in the global economic system, as the older system of borders and sovereign states is challenged by cross-border movements of capital, goods, and people. Regional trade groups like the North American Free Trade Agreement (NAFTA), supranational institutions like the European Union, global organizations like the United Nations, World Trade Organization (WTO), and International Monetary Fund (IMF), global corporations, nonstate militant groups, and terrorist organizations are all vying for power in the global system and operating through and around the borders of the traditional state.[34] However, contrary to Friedman's view, this has not led to equal access around the world. If it had, why would record numbers of people want to migrate? Contrary to Brown's view, it also has resulted not in a decline in state power but a reassertion of it, specifically through the construction of walls, fences, and other security apparatus at the border.[35] As the movement of people threatens their ability to control resources and populations, states around the world have responded by hardening borders and violently enforcing their authority. The hardening of borders represents a rearticulation and expansion, not a retreat, of state power.

The second indication that states retain their central role in the control of political space is the increased cooperation between states in the management of their borders. Most borders have ceased to be lines of dispute between states competing for control over territory. The situation on the Korean Peninsula, between Russia and Ukraine, and on the Line of Control in Kashmir notwithstanding, at many borders conflict has been replaced with cooperation as neighboring states work together against shared threats to their sovereign control over their territories.[36] States work together at the UN to recognize each other's sovereignty and reject secessionist and independence movements. States work together at borders to manage and regulate—to make legible to each other—people who do not acknowledge the state's exclusive right to control their territory: migrants, smugglers, and terrorists. There are many examples of these cross-border partnerships against shared threats. Morocco's crackdown on migrants, which was supported by funding from the European Union, included destroying migrant camps, detaining individuals, and constructing barbed-wire fences around Melilla and Ceuta. In December 2015, Turkey received EU funding to solidify its border and round up Syrian migrants attempting to move on to the European Union. The United States and Canada have many agreements that allow for the joint operation of border facilities, including US passport and customs checks in Canadian airports. The US and Mexican governments share information on drug smuggling at the border, and the United States supports Mexico's efforts to locate and detain migrants from other Central American countries before they reach the border.

These practices reinforce the primacy of the state through the regulation of the bodies of migrants, smugglers, and other unauthorized individuals. Restrictions on movement at borders are part of a long-term conflict between states and people who move, a conflict that goes back to the earliest states and human settlements. While the regulation of movement takes different forms through various historical periods, the underlying desire to protect privileges accrued through the control of resources and opportunities remains the same.

Chapter 4

The Global Poor

When Andrew Carnegie sold his vast holdings in the steel industry to J. P. Morgan in 1901 for $480 million (over $20 billion today), he was likely the wealthiest person in the world. His fortune was made during the Gilded Age, as the United States transitioned from a predominantly agricultural economy to become a global industrial power. Carnegie lived in New York, which was becoming one of the wealthiest cities in the world, and he advised US presidents Grover Cleveland, Benjamin Harrison, and William McKinley and Prime Minister William Gladstone in Britain. He dedicated the last years of his life to philanthropy; his legacy includes Carnegie Hall, Carnegie Mellon University, the Carnegie Endowment for Peace, and the Carnegie Corporation of New York. Scientists funded by his philanthropy discovered that the universe was expanding and proved DNA was genetic material, among many other advances. However, Carnegie, who migrated to the United States as a child for many of the same reasons motivating migrants today, was born into a completely different world.

Andrew Carnegie was born in Dunfermline, Scotland, in 1835. His father, William, was a handloom weaver who painstakingly produced textiles in his studio.[1] The Carnegie family lived in poverty in a tiny one-room flat above the studio that served as kitchen, living room, and bedroom all in one. The early 1800s were a period of rapid change in Europe that included unprecedented population growth, urbanization, and economic restructuring. While economic growth, a more varied diet, and advances in medicine and sanitation resulted in declining mortality rates, the cultural idea of restricting births had not taken hold and, as more children survived into adulthood, the population of Europe grew rapidly. Scotland's population increased by 40 percent from 1800 to 1830. At the same time, the Industrial Revolution introduced the ideas of mechanization and mass production, which allowed fewer workers to produce far more of a standardized product. The textile industry was at the leading edge of this transition.

These changes arrived on the Carnegies' doorstep only two years after Andrew was born. Artisans like William Carnegie made each article of clothing to order, usually by hand from start to finish by one person in a small shop. In the early 1830s, William's handloom weaving business briefly boomed because the labor-intensive products were desirable luxury items. The Panic of 1837, which begin as a financial crisis in the United States and resulted in an extended recession, destroyed the market for handwoven textiles, causing unemployment to soar and wages to decline in Dunfermline. The weaving businesses that survived the downturn in the early 1840s were those that used the more efficient power loom; however, Carnegie's father did not make the switch. Meanwhile, the growing population and the lack of traditional jobs led to mass unemployment in rural areas across Europe and drove people to the cities. In 1800, England was 20 percent urban; by 1890 it was 60 percent. London's population grew from 1 million in 1800 to 2.5 million in 1850. Some rural immigrants found jobs in the new factories, but many more lived in squalor in the slums of London—their lives are documented in Charles Dickens's portraits of dingy, brutal street life in the 1840s. There were epidemics of typhoid, measles, and influenza. Carnegie's sister, Anne, was born in 1840 but died in 1842.

Penniless and without any job prospects in Scotland, in 1848 Carnegie's mother secured a loan from a friend and paid the family's fare on a ship to America. The Irish Potato Famine was at its height in 1848, and there were so many immigrants that year that many different types of ships were used; they became known as "coffin ships" because so many people died on the way. The fifty-day journey across the Atlantic was arduous and dangerous. There were too many migrants on the ships, no privacy, and rarely enough food. The Carnegies' was a converted whaling vessel that did not have enough crew, so the seasick passengers were often roused from their misery to help out with the work. Thirty million migrants from Europe traveled to the United States from 1815 to 1915.[2] Between 1851 and 1861, 600,000 migrants arrived in Australia.[3]

The Carnegies were undocumented immigrants when they arrived at the docks of New York City that summer; the United Kingdom did not yet provide passports in the 1840s and would not for another seventy years. They took advantage of their undocumented status to lie about their ages, adding a few years to Andrew's and shaving a few off William's in order to make themselves more attractive to employers. The family had relatives in the Pittsburgh area, so they settled there to begin a new life. In America, the teenage Andrew Carnegie found opportunity and encouragement for his ambition. He was hired as a messenger boy for a telegraph company and quickly rose through the ranks to become a telegraph operator. Only a few years after arriving, the young man wrote to an uncle in Scotland that he was certainly much better off in America: "If I had been in Dunfermline working at the loom it is very likely I would have been a poor weaver all my days, but here I can certainly do something better than that."[4] Carnegie used his role as telegraph operator to develop connections with the owners of the railroad companies. Under the tutelage of these capitalists, he slowly invested his earnings in new businesses related to the railroads. During the Civil War his investments in steel became extremely profitable and he focused his attention on the emerging industry. After the war, his company, US Steel, grew into an industrial powerhouse that fueled industrial growth in America and filled Carnegie's pockets with millions of dollars. His one great failure late in life was his inability to give away all of his wealth before he died. He tried earnestly, but it was too much; instead he founded the Carnegie Corporation to continue to "do real and permanent good." Almost a century after his death, it is still one of the major philanthropic organizations in the United States.

The global poor, then and now

In the past decade, millions of families have faced similar choices to the Carnegies' as their ways of life were threatened by economic and political changes that forced them to leave their homes in search of better opportunities elsewhere. Migrants today are escaping poor living conditions and job prospects, a side effect of rapid rural-to-urban migration in their home countries—just as the Carnegies did a century and a half earlier in Scotland.[5] The population of the African continent was 336 million in 1970; it is 1.1 billion today. Migrants today step onto cramped, unseaworthy boats to cross the Mediterranean to Europe or the Indian Ocean to Australia without enough food, water, or crew to operate the ships, on voyages similar to what the Carnegies endured. Whether they're fleeing the Irish Potato Famine or the Syrian civil war, the migrants lack documents that would guarantee their ability to cross borders and arrive in the new countries with little more than a desire for a new life.

There are also clear differences. In Carnegie's time, despite the existence of slums in cities like London, Europe was already the wealthiest place in the world, a feat achieved by extracting resources from colonies. Today's poor countries do not have colonies to exploit and have to contend with wealthy countries that maintain control over most international institutions, such as the World Bank and International Monetary

Fund.[6] Furthermore, population increases in decolonized countries today have been far more drastic. London's population increased from 1 to 2.5 million people from 1800 to 1850, while the population of Lagos, Nigeria, increased from 290,000 in 1950 to 23 million in 2015.[7] In the nineteenth century, the ideas of citizenship and identity documents were only just beginning to emerge; settler colonies in the Americas, Australia, or Africa were looking for more people to help seize control of land and then to work it. Most significantly, when industrialization restructured the economies of agricultural regions in Europe, it left unemployed rural workers free to board boats overseas. Today, by contrast, there are no countries open to large-scale migration. Without an outlet for excess labor, the only option for unemployed rural populations is to live in an urban slum. Today one out of every six people in the world lives in a slum—more than 1 billion people.

The Carnegie family's migration experience came during a historically unique transition in how states settled the poor. According to political scientist David Forsyth, "At the beginning of the nineteenth century an estimated three-quarters of all people alive were trapped in bondage against their will either in some form of slavery or serfdom."[8] As these practices were gradually abolished, Europe's population grew, and the establishment of settler colonies created new demands for labor, a brief window opened in which the poor of Europe were encouraged to migrate to new homes. Even while this mass migration was beginning, the seeds of the current restrictions on the movement of the poor were sown in the new constitutions of states, which created limits and regulations that would resettle the poor and lock them in place. Similar to slavery and serfdom in the past, the creation of a legal regime of citizenship and identity documents, combined with new border infrastructure, resulted in a global border regime to restrict the movement of the poor and control labor.

Slavery, serfdom, and the privilege of movement

Prior to the emergence of states, people were free to move as they pleased. As states created legal systems, beginning with oral codes and, later, written documents such as the Magna Carta and the French and American constitutions, the right to move has been addressed in different ways, with some movements restricted and others allowed. For most poor people living in states, movement was impossible due to their status as slaves or serfs, or for fear of being accused of vagrancy. In early legal documents the right to move was typically limited to the elite—lords and nobles—and merchants who traded in the goods they desired.[9]

Most early states were built on slavery and indentured servitude; the practice was significant in the development of states through the earliest democracies, including the United States. Formal slavery was uncommon in Europe by the fifteenth century, although European states did continue to use slavery in their colonies abroad. Nevertheless, many laws were in place to restrict the movement of former slaves, serfs, and indentured servants. The social and economic systems of the day restricted the movement of the poor by chaining them to rural farms and mines through unpayable debts or simply the cruelty of the whip. In medieval England, for example, law professor William Quigley estimates that two-thirds of the population "lived in a virtual state of slavery; they worked for the lord and in return received support from the lord, but in effect they were the property of the lord, who could dispose of them by sale or gift."[10]

The Magna Carta is an example of an early legal document that established the right to free movement for a portion of the population. The Magna Carta emerged out of a peace treaty that was signed at Runnymede in Surrey, England, by King John in 1215 in the aftermath of a rebellion by lords and nobles.[11] The document establishes the limits of the relationship between the king and the nobles and is most often cited today for the clauses that guaranteed the rights of habeas corpus and a swift trial. It also includes several clauses describing the rights of nobles and merchants to "enter or leave England unharmed and without fear, and ... stay or travel within it, by land or water, for purposes of trade, free from all illegal exactions, in accordance with ancient and lawful customs."[12] The document makes clear that merchants can come in and out of England to sell goods, and that nobles are free to travel as long as they remain allied with the kingdom. The Magna Carta did not limit the movement of the poor; it simply did not consider it. It assumed that the poor were attached to feudal estates as serfs; travel would be as an attendant and property of a noble.[13]

In England, poor laws prevented laborers from moving to new jurisdictions.[14] The earliest of these laws followed the Black Death, which killed over one-quarter of the population and made it possible for laborers to demand higher wages. In response, the Ordinance of Labourers of 1345/1350 and following statutes required all able-bodied men to work and punished those who "fled" their place of labor or went to look for work elsewhere. The Statute of Cambridge of 1388 required laborers to have a letter of permission from their manor lord allowing them to travel.[15] The Vagabonds and Beggars Act of 1495 put the poor in jail for several days before sending them back to where they last lived or were born. The Vagabonds Act of 1547 was one of the cruelest and called for two years of jail and the branding of a V on their bodies as a penalty, something that was not widely carried out. These acts also required the local manors and parishes to set up work for these people and to provide basic aid for the elderly or infirm who could not work. The overriding result of these acts was to limit the ability of the poor to move and to confine them to their home towns.

In the US, slavery continued in the South through the Civil

War. Even after emancipation in 1865, many former slaves were subjected to forced labor for decades. Vagrancy laws were used to limit the movement of former slaves and provide cheap labor for former enslavers. Douglas Blackmon's *Slavery by Another Name* describes how this process worked.[16] Across the rural South, justices of the peace looked for African Americans moving through their area, often on train tracks, and then charged them with vagrancy. When they could not pay the fine, the accused would be sentenced to six months or a year in jail. A local farmer could pay off the fine and the accused would then be compelled go to their farm and work for them until the amount was repaid. Typically the conditions were horrible: prisoners were chained overnight, underfed, and viciously punished if they showed any signs of resistance. Often, toward the end of the prisoner's sentence, the farmer would accuse them of an additional crime and the justice of the peace would extend their sentence. Later, coal mines and steel mills, including some owned by Carnegie's US Steel, became large players in the prisoner labor market as well. Blackmon argues that, in essence, slavery continued in this manner through the early twentieth century as African Americans who dared to try to move around were captured, accused of vagrancy, and sent back into slavery for years at a time.

Citizenship: Identifying who belongs

As the violent restrictions of slavery, serfdom, and vagrancy laws were lifted in the early modern era, a brief period followed of relatively free movement for the poor of Europe. But a new system of citizenship and identity documents was soon implemented. The formalization of the state as a legal regime played a key role in this process. From the earliest states through the present day, a primary function of the state has been to create a system to locate and control the movement of the population and manage access to resources and territory. Although states have existed for several thousand years, the idea that the state controls a territory, defined as a bounded space of exclusive administration by the state, is relatively new.[17] Prior to the sixteenth century, cartography was limited and it was not possible for mapmakers to create a detailed, mathematically accurate representation of the state's space. Earlier states, such as ancient Chinese states or even the Roman Empire, controlled land and excluded other people with walls and military force, but they did not have the conceptual idea of a bounded territorial space that was exclusively governed by the state through laws and sovereignty. The modern notion of territory emerged as local lords gained control over everyday economic and political decisions from the Catholic Church in the sixteenth century. The treaties of Westphalia (1648) formally separated everyday economic and political authority from spiritual authority, over the objections of the Pope. The result, which was written out by the scholar Gottfried Leibniz in the late 1600s, was separate territories of jurisdiction for kings over the everyday lives of their people, recognition of these jurisdictions by other kings, and a separate spiritual realm governed by the Pope in Rome.

From the seventeenth century onward, as the connection between the state and a bounded, defined territory grew stronger, the rulers in these newly emergent jurisdictional territories in Europe worked to create an ordered set of knowledge that allowed the land, resources, and people to be governed.[18] One way to conceive of these state-ordering practices is through the metaphors of legibility and vision.[19] In order to govern, the state needs to be able to see the people, the land, and the resources in its territory in a legible or nameable way; they must be quantifiable and situated in a known, locatable place. This might involve surveying the land and mapping resources or settling populations and performing censuses so that labor can be located, crops can be taxed, and soldiers can be conscripted when needed. Scholars use the term *governmentality* to describe these state practices, which create the bureaucracy of government that gathers information about the population, resources, and territory through surveillance—the counting, mapping, and locating strategies that make the population known to the state, allowing them to be governed.[20] These ordering practices require more careful monitoring of the population. The first step of this monitoring is to know where the population actually is.

In the nineteenth and twentieth centuries, after the end of the serf-and-lord model, citizenship emerged as a key mechanism for states to locate and control access to land and resources. By creating citizenship as a new category of belonging, states divided and organized people into insiders who belonged and outsiders who did not. Identity documents and passports made these differences, which were not based on visible characteristics like race, legible to the state bureaucracy. The exact definition of citizenship has varied across history and geography, but generally involves membership in a political community that confers rights on the member and includes obligations to participate in and protect that community.[21] From its early origins through the present day, citizenship has always been a two-sided concept, with the state guaranteeing rights for some people while excluding many others from the right to have rights.

The Classical Athenian form of citizenship was limited to men born to city natives, and the ability to exercise their franchise was dependent on the free time afforded them through the work of women and slaves denied a political voice. It is estimated that Athens had 40,000 citizens and 90,000 slaves. Political scientist Richard Bellamy writes that for critics of the Greek notion of citizenship, "[i]n reality, it was doubly oppressive. On the one hand, it rested on the oppression of slaves, women, and other non-citizens. On the other hand, it was oppressive of citizens demanding they sacrifice their private interests to the service of the state."[22] The Roman Empire offered citizenship to the residents of conquered lands, but this was only a guarantee of equal protection under the law, not a role in decision-making within the state. As with many ancient ideas, the concept of citizenship was unused during the Middle Ages and did not reemerge until the seventeenth and eighteenth centuries, as political theorists began to write about the limits of the authority of monarchies and the possibility of a state governed through a social contract with the people.[23] While Thomas Hobbes saw humans as self-interested and needing a state to protect them from other people, John Locke worried about the possibility for excesses if the state had too much power.[24] Prior to this era, monarchies enjoyed mostly unchecked sovereign authority, but the wealthy elite, on whom the monarchs relied for capital and militias, were demanding more influence over the decisions of the state.

The American and French revolutions in 1776 and 1789 brought these debates about the relationship between the state and citizens to a head. The discussion about how far the new idea of citizenship should extend revolved around two issues. The first was whether there are universal human rights that apply to everyone globally, or whether rights are embedded in the relationship between an individual and a state. The second issue was whether the protections guaranteed by these states should be granted equally to all people within the state's territorial boundaries or whether states should be able to differentiate between citizens, noncitizen residents, and foreign subjects.

Views on this were widely divergent. For example, in France, the Enlightenment thinker Nicolas de Condorcet wrote in his 1790 text *On the Admission of Women to the Rights of Citizenship* that "either no individual of the human species has any true rights, or all have the same; and he or she who votes against the rights of another, whatever may be his or her religion, colour, or sex, has by that fact abjured his own."[25] But

Condorcet's view that all people had equal rights did not win the day; the constitutions of France and the United States both included substantial qualifications on who had the rights of a citizen. In France, the 1789 Declaration of the Rights of Man and Citizen was approved just five days after the Bill of Rights was passed in the United States. The two documents mark a shift: sovereignty was no longer the divine right of kings but placed in the hands of the people.[26] The Declaration of the Rights of Man and Citizen emphasizes that all men are born free and are equal in rights. However, it establishes a different category of citizen in the nation for the administration of sovereignty within the territory. Property owners were "active citizens" in the nation, possessed the right to vote, and were completely protected by the law. A second category, "passive citizen," was a more limited definition that allowed women, those under twenty-five, and foreigners to be excluded from full citizenship in France.

The 1791 French constitution institutionalized the Declaration, as has every succeeding French constitution through the present Fifth Republic. The US Constitution also guaranteed rights to citizens using the lofty prose of universal rights, but simultaneously limited the rights of large portions of the population by denying the vote to women and perpetuating the institution of slavery. If the state grants equal rights to all of humanity, then there is no way to justify keeping slaves. However, if citizenship is granted only to select individuals who are born within the state and support it through taxes on their property, this creates other classes of individuals who may be within the state's borders but are not covered equally under the law. These categories allow the flexibility to differentiate between citizens, foreign visitors, and, at least for a time, slaves or other indentured servants. The category for slaves was eventually abolished, but the distinction between citizen and noncitizen remains, and the constitutions of newly independent countries continued to incorporate these distinct categories and reserve the majority of rights for citizens, not all humans.

These foundational documents of democracy are more conservative than they first appear. They essentially transfer authority from the king to the nobles and wealthy landowners of the state, not to the population generally.[27] Consequently, they are consistent with the longer history of the state, which guards the wealth of the elite while relying on the majority of the population for troops and labor.

Identity documents

The institution of citizenship put in place a system for identifying where people belong based on birthplace. "On the global scale, citizenship is an immensely powerful instrument of social closure," writes sociologist Rogers Brubaker in *Nation and National Identity*. "It shields prosperous and peaceful states from the great majority of those who—in a world without borders and exclusive citizenries—would seek to flee war, civil strife, famine, joblessness, or environmental degradation, or who would move in the hope of securing greater opportunities for their children."[28] In the past, movement was regulated based on identifiable characteristics of race or allowed primarily for those who possessed substantial wealth. With modern citizenship, the only way to establish and monitor who possesses citizenship is through documents such as passports.[29] John Torpey, author of *The Invention of the Passport*, notes, "In the late 1800s, governments became increasingly oriented to making distinctions between their own citizens/subjects and others, a distinction that could be made only on the basis of documents."[30] In the twentieth century, state bureaucracies such as border patrols, customs agents, and naturalization services were developed that used new technologies such as photographs, fingerprints, and bar codes for more intensive monitoring of the population. These were carried out through new efforts to count and document the population through censuses and birth certificates.[31]

By the turn of the twentieth century, anti-immigration sentiment was growing in many settler-colonial states as residents gained wealth and privilege and began to fear the changes new migrants would bring. In the United States, for example, books such as G. G. Rupert's *The Yellow Peril* (1911) and tabloid newspaper stories spread fear that people of Asian origin represented a threat to the white racial character of the United States. By the time the Statue of Liberty in New York was dedicated in 1886, its inscription was already beginning to ring hollow:

> Give me your tired, your poor,
> Your huddled masses, yearning to breathe free,
> The wretched refuse of your teeming shore,
> Send these, the homeless, tempest-tost to me.
> I lift my lamp beside the golden door.

Four years earlier, Congress had passed the Chinese Exclusion Act, which completely banned Chinese laborers and prevented people of Chinese ancestry already present in the United States from becoming citizens. It also "excluded convicts, lunatics, idiots, and persons likely to become public charges"[32] and was not repealed until 1943. The Immigration Act of 1924 established quotas for immigration based on nationality, which encouraged Western European migration at the expense of Eastern and Southern Europeans and Asians. Although the specifics of the regulations have changed, the United States has continued to restrict immigration based on quotas ever since. The current system is rooted in the 1965 amendments to the Immigration and Nationality Act, which abolished nationality quotas in favor of hemisphere quotas and caps on individual countries. Initially these caps were 170,000 from the Eastern Hemisphere and 120,000 from the Western, with a limit of

20,000 per country. Over the ensuing decades these quotas were increased to 700,000 total and favor relatives of current citizens and permanent residents. The US president has the discretion to admit a set number of refugees each year. In 2016, the cap was 85,000; in 2017 it will be raised to 100,000.

The other settler-colonial states, such as Australia, Canada, and New Zealand, instituted similar restrictions throughout the twentieth century. Canada restricted non-European migration into the 1960s. In Australia, the 1901 Immigration Restriction Act limited Asian immigration. It came to be known as the White Australia policy and was not repealed until 1971. Since then, Australia has a nondiscriminatory immigration system, but it still restricts the total number of migrants. In 1992, the government implemented a mandatory detention policy that requires all migrants suspected of violating Australia's immigration laws to be held until their status can be adjudicated. The Border Protection Bill of 2001 gave the Australian government the right to remove ships suspected of ferrying migrants from its territorial seas. These are held in detention facilities in Nauru or returned to other neighboring states including East Timor, Malaysia, and Papua New Guinea, as discussed in chapter 3.

The growing importance of citizenship and the development of new documents to identify the population coincided with changes in the perception of foreigners that resulted in increasingly strict monitoring of movements at borders.[33] As states began to offer more services, such as health care, welfare, and housing, to their populations in the early twentieth century, there was concern that noncitizens could take advantage. The fear of spies and other foreign agents played a particularly important role in establishing the passport system. Prior to World War I, the only time passports were required was in times of war, to ensure that enemy agents or sympathizers could be located and prevented from entering the state. There were forms of passports during the French

Revolution, the US Civil War, and World War I. In Europe, the passport system was retained after the end of World War I, marking the first time they were required during a period of peace. In 1920, the newly established League of Nations held the Paris Conference on Passports and Customs Formalities and Through Tickets to standardize the practice between member states. The United States did not have a peacetime passport requirement until after World War II. In 1980, the United Nations held a conference that led to a global standard of machine-readable passports. In the past decade, biometric passports with radio-frequency identification (RFID) chips that store data on the traveler's appearance, birthplace, and citizenship have been adopted.[34] These changes combine to create a system that allows states to identify individuals based on their citizenship and restrict access based on place-based categories of belonging.

The global border regime

The Carnegie family, and the millions of other poor migrants who crowded onto rickety and repurposed boats for long and dangerous journeys in search of better lives in the nineteenth century, did so during a unique moment of transition in the relationship between states and the poor. In the centuries before the great nineteenth-century migration, the relationship between wealth and movement was primarily established within individual states, not between them. As late as 1700, wealth was spread relatively evenly around the world, with the wealthiest states wealthier than the poorest by only single-digit percentages.[35] Inequality was more evident within each state. In the twentieth century, the same paradigm of the wealthy controlling movement and opportunity returned, but in a new configuration. Slavery was abolished, the constitutions of most states guarantee freedom of movement within

85

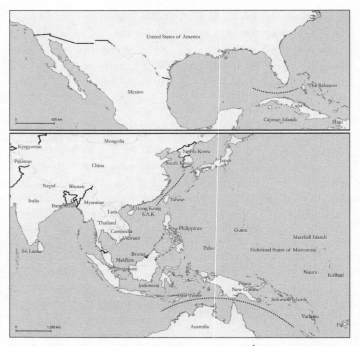

Border barriers around the world. Data from Élisabeth Vallet and Stéphane Rosière.

the state, and the right to free internal movement within a country was codified in the Universal Declaration of Human Rights, adopted by the United Nations General Assembly in 1948. Countries that do impose internal movement restrictions are considered human-rights violators, such as Myanmar, which limits the movement of the Rohingya minority group, and China, which limits rural-to-urban migration through the Hukou system that denies benefits to rural residents in cities.

The ability of the majority of the people in the world to move freely, access opportunities, and participate in political decisions is still severely restricted—but now these restrictions are maintained *between* states rather than within them.[36]

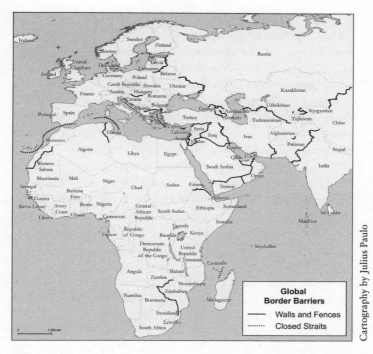

Cartography by Julius Paulo

While there are still substantial wealth gaps between the rich and the poor within countries, colonialism and capitalism have combined to produce phenomenal differences in wealth between states. Today, Qatar and Norway have the highest per-capita GDPs, approximately $97,000, while the Democratic Republic of Congo has the lowest at $300.[37] An average worker in Norway makes in one day what a worker in the Congo makes in a year. These wealth gaps, combined with a new round of demographic and economic change in many former colonial states, are driving a new global migration as the poor look for better opportunities elsewhere.

In the twenty-first century, there are not any open settler colonies looking for workers. Globally, movement between states is restricted by documents based on birthplace that protect privilege and contain labor: the global border regime.[38] As citizenship documents and border crossing procedures have been formalized, the movement of the poor is limited again—just as it was by slavery and indentured servitude in previous eras—through laws that restrict movement based on different classes of people and violence that targets those who disregard the laws. As migrants are denied the legal right to move, many look for other ways to cross borders, often through the vast and poorly guarded spaces between crossing points.

What is new in the past twenty years is that many states have also begun to focus on irregular movements in the in-between spaces of the border. As late as 1990, only fifteen countries had walls or fences on their borders. At the beginning of 2016, almost seventy did. In 2015 alone, countries as diverse as Austria, Bulgaria, Estonia, Hungary, Kenya, Saudi Arabia, Slovenia, and Tunisia proposed or began construction of border walls.[39] The violence of borders goes hand in hand with protecting the privileges that borders created. Rather than an open border and access to opportunities, the potential Andrew Carnegies of today are met with the full violence of the state: barbed wire, drones, and militarized agents that prevent them from moving.

Chapter 5

Maps, Hedges, and Fences: Enclosing the Commons and Bounding the Seas

John Reynolds, who came to lead the largest peasant rebellion in the history of England, was a tinker by trade. Today we mostly use the term *tinker* to mean "to fiddle with something," which turns out to be exactly what tinkers did. They were traveling repairmen who would fix household items by tinkering with them. The details of how Reynolds was transformed from a tinker into the mythical Captain Pouch who led the Midlands Revolt of 1607 have—sadly—been lost to history. He must have been a persuasive speaker, because he convinced his followers that the pouch he always carried at his side contained "sufficient matter to defend them against all comers."[1]

For a while, the powerful contents of Reynolds's pouch remained secret and apparently worked as promised. The revolt began in 1607 at the May Eve celebrations and within a few weeks it spread through Northamptonshire, Warwickshire, and Leicestershire. Previous peasant revolts in England had tended to be small, including a few dozen protestors at the most. Captain Pouch was able to rally thousands of people, including many women and children. There were 3,000 people at Hillmorton, Warwickshire, and an astounding 5,000 at Cotesbach, which was approximately 10 percent of the entire population of the county of Leicestershire at the time.[2]

Whatever image you have in your mind of a "rebel" does not match Reynolds and his fellow Diggers and Levellers, as they called themselves. They were surprisingly well behaved. Reynolds instructed his followers "not to swear, nor to offer violence to any person, but to ply their business and make fair works."[3] They did not kill people or carry out traditional attacks. They did not rape and pillage. They did not steal anything. Although King James I (who reigned from 1603 to 1625) was forced to raise a militia against them, they were not even rebelling against the king. Instead, they were petitioning him to enforce his own laws, which local lords were breaking. Above all, the rebels gardened: they would meet at a field in order to dig up and level recently planted hedges and fill in ditches.

Captain Pouch's rebels were drawn from the peasants and laborers whose livelihoods were disrupted by the introduction of the new system of private property in England during the sixteenth, seventeenth, and eighteenth centuries, as the feudal system gave way to agrarian capitalism, which over the following centuries would displace the vast majority of rural laborers and send them into the slums of London, Manchester, Liverpool, and beyond looking for work. Although this transition eventually resulted in massive population movements, the original purpose of the enclosures was to limit peasants' movement and restrict their access to what had been common lands for grazing animals, gathering wood, and planting subsistence crops. The agricultural system of the sixteenth century was hierarchical and maintained wealth in the hands of a few, but it also provided space for peasants to grind out a living off the land. Peasants could not move freely over long distances, but they could move freely through the forests and common fields of the local area. Captain Pouch and his rebels rose up against the enclosure of these spaces to protect their access to common lands.

The factors that led to the Midlands Revolt in 1607 illustrate how the power to control the land was captured through the imposition of boundaries and how this transformed the relationship between humans and the environment. This relationship continued to transform in the centuries after the revolt, as states claimed the land of the earth as sovereign territories and, in the twentieth century, enclosed the oceans as the exclusive economic zones of states. The foundations of movement restrictions at borders today are based on earlier events such as the Midlands Revolt against enclosure; the 1648 treaties of Westphalia, which ended the Thirty Years' War; the 1884 Berlin Conference, which partitioned Africa into European colonies; and the creation of the Law of the Sea in 1994, each of which expanded the ability of states to control access to land, resources, and opportunities.

Enclosing resources

The conflict between the human desires to wander and to settle began with the emergence of sedentary agriculture, around 10,000 BCE. As some communities settled, it became necessary to protect their resources from other mobile populations. These settlements grew, as greater numbers provided better protection in raids and were necessary to carry out large irrigation and construction projects. Eventually, these developed into early states around 3000 BCE in Egypt and Mesopotamia, although they were more rudimentary than modern states, lacking boundaries, a clear territory, and codified legal regimes. What they shared with modern states were systems of organizing power to obtain more resources. Consequently, early states were always pushing up against neighboring areas in search of more labor and agricultural land.

Modern histories of states emphasize the positive attributes of state expansion: a stable source of food, an orderly society, protection in the form of an army and city walls and, later, opportunities such as education, health care, and jobs. Many characterized interactions between the state and outsiders as a contrast between civilization and barbarity, but we know this version because states write their histories from their perspective, while many mobile peoples did not record their experiences.[4] The positive version of state expansion ignores the significant role of coercion in state-making. States extracted taxes that were used to pay for armies, administration, and large building projects. States were also incubators for disease, with a dense population, monoculture crops, and the pests that follow. Most states practiced slavery and relied on forced labor and military conscription for territorial expansion.

Walls and fences are among the oldest and most familiar technologies rulers and states use to prevent undesired movement into and out of their area of control: for example, the Great Wall of China, Hadrian's Wall, and walls around medieval cities in Europe.[5] For early city-states, walls provided a number of advantages. Economically, they funneled traffic into the city through gates to allow monitoring and taxing of goods. Militarily, walls provided a line to defend the resources and people of the city. Symbolically, they were a visual representation of the power of the city or state. However, their effectiveness was uneven. The long walls the Chinese built were largely failures because they were easy to get around and hard to guard properly. Although they are more technologically sophisticated, many of the new walls built in the past twenty years suffer from these same vulnerabilities.[6] However, shorter walls, like those around medieval cities or around prisons today, can be very effective if properly guarded.

Ancient walls are an early example of the concept of territoriality, "the attempt by an individual or group to affect influence or control people, phenomena and relationships by delimiting and asserting control over a geographical area."[7] Human territoriality differs from animal territoriality in that it is not an instinct but a strategy, something that can be turned on and off. Territoriality involves classifying a particular area through a claim, communicating that claim to others, and then enforcing the claim with a system that limits access to the area through movement restrictions or violence. The advantage of a territorial strategy is that it reifies power by making it visible but impersonal. It demonstrates the claim while deflecting attention from the individual or group who is making it. This is particularly evident in property law today, where it is not one individual who is excluding another individual from a particular land: the authority is scaled up to the legal regime as a whole.[8] Simply making a map or stating a claim to a particular place is not sufficient to control it. The crucial aspect is the physical act of limiting access to the place. Once movement into a place is controlled and individuals are excluded, territoriality is in effect.

Prior to the modern era, much of the land in the world lay outside the exclusive control of emergent states. Beyond those city walls, the authority, knowledge, and influence of the rulers declined precipitously. James C. Scott, author of *The Art of Not Being Governed*, put it this way: "To an eye not yet hypnotized by archeological remains and state-centric histories, the landscape would have seemed virtually all periphery and no centers. Nearly all the population and territory were outside [the states'] ambit."[9] Today, by contrast, from the moment an individual is born to the moment they die, they live in a multitude of overlapping bounded spaces that affect every aspect of their existence. These lines include international borders, state boundaries, county boundaries, city boundaries, city council districts, police precincts, fire-station districts, school districts, electricity grids, trash-collection areas, neighborhood boards, gated communities, and private properties. The list goes on. Although many of these lines are invisible and permeable, they affect quality of life in terms of the availability of public education, infrastructure, government benefits like health care or Social Security, the right to free speech, and access to the economic opportunities.

Boundaries emerged from the efforts by states and rulers to enclose land and resources by limiting the movement of other people. In the sixteenth and seventeenth centuries, as capitalism took hold in Europe, lords began to enclose common fields and forests and convert them into bounded, owned, private properties. As these new enclosures were enforced, Captain Pouch's rebels and others who were affected by them rose up to resist.

Private property and the Midlands Revolt

At the core of the Midlands Revolt were questions over access to land and the right to control it that are still debated today. What rights should people have to use lands? How can traditional uses be reconciled with the exclusive rights of a property owner? How can improvements made by one individual or organization be protected from others? To what extent should the exclusive uses of one group be allowed to harm others nearby?

Private property today consists of a series of rights that are guaranteed by the government in perpetuity.[10] These rights include the ability to use land, keep others out, mine it, or lease it out.[11] Governments retain some rights over what can be done on a property through zoning laws, environmental laws, and labor laws. If an individual fails to pay taxes on the property or violates these other laws the property can revert to the government or be resold to another individual, but generally landowners are free to use the land as they see fit.

During the Middle Ages, the modern idea of private property did not exist. A wide range of different relationships between kings, vassals, peasants, and the church regulated land use.[12] In medieval England, the king claimed sovereignty over all of the land and leased it out to vassals, or lords, who pledged military aid to the king and provided a small portion of their harvests as a tax. All of the land was ultimately the king's. The manors of the lords were relatively isolated, since populations were smaller and movement was difficult before the existence of modern transportation technologies. This meant that each manor was largely self-contained and produced a wide range of goods necessary for subsistence. The area around the manor home was divided into different sections, depending on the productivity of the land. In the English Midlands, the best farmlands were cleared and used for crops in an open-field system.[13] The residents of a village shared the lands by allocating different strips to farmers each year. Farmers had strips in many different parts of the lands, so no one monopolized the most productive areas. The manor also had wastes— uncultivated brush lands—and forests nearby for grazing animals and collecting firewood and other forest products.[14] The peasants did not own these lands but had access to them to farm, hunt, raise animals, and gather fuel. These commons were essential for their survival and provided them with some freedom to roam. The lord made a profit on the arrangement; the peasants had autonomy to use the common lands for their own purposes. For the king, the system provided access to a militia when necessary, raised taxes, and kept the commoners settled and occupied.

The use of common lands by all free men, a customary practice for centuries, was enshrined in the Magna Carta as well as by the Charter of the Forest, which stated that "All forests that have been created in our reign shall at once be disafforested. River-banks that have been enclosed in our reign shall be treated similarly." In this context, *disafforested* does not mean "deforested," but that limits on access to forests were to be removed. Furthermore, in the document, *forest* is used to refer to any lands that were not developed, whether actual forests, wilds, grasslands and moors, or riverbanks that were used to pasture sheep. In later versions of the Magna Carta, beginning in 1217, these forest-related clauses were separated out and expanded on in the Charter of the Forest, which reiterated the right of all free men to use and access the forest so long as it did not harm their neighbors.[15] Over the centuries, these documents were reaffirmed by successive kings. They were not completely replaced until the nineteenth and twentieth centuries, when Parliament formalized the legal regime of the modern state. The founding documents of England guaranteed the protection of and access to the commons.

Although the enclosure of common lands would hypothetically provide larger yields from fields and more tax revenues for the monarchy, English kings were largely against the practice. They issued over a dozen restrictions on it from the fifteenth through seventeenth centuries, beginning with the anti-enclosure acts of 1489 and 1516, which sought to discourage it by imposing fines and heavy taxes—often half of all profits—on lords who enclosed their lands. The kings' primary concern was not necessarily for the well-being of the peasants. They were afraid of the potential movement of poor people that would result from the enclosure of common lands, and that peasants displaced by enclosure could become paupers or vagrants who would overwhelm the fledgling cities of the time and pose a threat to the reign of the king. That fear proved to be well-founded when widespread enclosure displaced the vast majority of the rural poor in the eighteenth and nineteenth centuries, driving mass migration to settler colonies around the world. From the king's perspective, it was better to restrict the poor to manors by allowing them access to forests and fields for subsistence, which simultaneously maintained their debt and dependence on the local lord.

In the years preceding the Midlands Revolt, four significant changes combined to upset the traditional relationship that tied peasants to the land.[16] First, and least decisively, population growth strained older, inefficient subsistence-agriculture techniques, creating food shortages. Second, with the rise of capitalism, agricultural goods were beginning to be seen as a commodity that could be sold for a profit, not simply as necessities to sustain life: forests could be converted to croplands for grain or, more frequently, pasture for sheep to produce wool. Third, Henry VIII's dissolution of the monasteries in 1539 transferred large holdings from the church to laymen.[17] Finally, in the sixteenth century, modern maps transformed how people could visualize the landscape.

P. D. A. Harvey, a historian of cartography, writes that "in the England of 1500 maps were little understood or used. By 1600 they were familiar objects of everyday life"[18] and had been accepted as a representation of reality due to new techniques in surveying and cartography.[19] These included the introduction of scale, isometric drawing, and the printing press, which allowed maps to be made and distributed more widely and affordably.[20] "Far more than a revolution in the ways maps were made, it was a revolution in the ways of thought of those who used them," Harvey writes.[21]

Beyond the obvious military uses, the revolution in cartography and "ways of thought" affected how landlords managed their lands.[22] The practice of surveying manors emerged in the fifteenth century, but early surveys did not include maps. Instead, they described in precise prose the extent of a manor, relying on geographic features of the land.[23] By the late sixteenth century the lords possessed new maps with lines that precisely marked the boundaries of their lands.

The significance of these changes cannot be overstated. Up until the sixteenth century in England, land was conceived of as a space that might be controlled by someone but did not necessarily belong to anyone besides the king. But once surveyors and mapmakers codified the rural agricultural land of England, it became less a vast space people knew through local experience and more a disciplined commodity, captured on paper and administered from a distance. It was no longer necessary to have local knowledge; land was legible to anyone who could see the map—an elite group that was often limited to the monarchy, the lords, and their agents.[24]

For Captain Pouch and his rebels, the idea of property manifested through the creation of enclosures and the planting of hedges, which became the focal point of protests. Maps made visual the abstract idea of property, but hedges and fences allowed a new form of control over space to materialize on the ground.[25] As they were planted and grown, hedges were a stark visual reminder that the older land uses were changing and the lord was establishing firmer control. The visual impact on the landscape was dramatic. Panoramic views were closed off and bounded territories materialized where open fields and wastes had been previously.

The Midlands Revolt started at spring festivals in 1607, when people gathered to celebrate but also to complain about the new restrictions on access to common forests. In Northamptonshire, the two primary landlords were the Treshams of Rushton Hall, a long-established Catholic family that had fallen on hard times, and the Montagus of Boughton House, who were nouveau riche. In the years preceding, the Treshams had been aggressively enclosing their lands in order to shore up their finances, while Lord Montagu had given a speech in Parliament in support of the peasants. In addition to targeting the Treshams' hedges at Rushton, Captain Pouch and his rebels also destroyed Sir Euseby Isham's enclosures at Pytchley in Northamptonshire. The revolt spread to neighboring Warwickshire and Leicestershire in May of 1607.

The rebels emphasized that their cause was not against the king, but the actions of the lords in violation of the king's laws. However, although the law discouraged the enclosures, the threat of a mass movement against the hierarchical class system was more troublesome than the violations of the law. Under pressure from the king, Lord Montagu, as the deputy lieutenant and high sheriff of Northamptonshire, was ordered to raise a militia to put down the rebellion. This placed Montagu in the unenviable position of facing down the peasants he sympathized with, who were targeting land claimed by a relative of his nearby rivals, the Treshams of Rushton Hall.

The Midlands Revolt culminated at the edge of Rockingham Forest on June 8, 1607, in Newton, Northamptonshire, on the lands of Sir Thomas Tresham's nephew, also named Thomas Tresham. Lord Montagu arrived with a militia he had raised from among his own servants at Boughton House and the households of other local gentry, because the local men refused to participate. Lord Montagu read a proclamation from the king, but the Diggers continued their work, perhaps buoyed by the fact that Captain Pouch's magical pouch had protected them so far or hoping that the sympathetic Lord Montagu would not use violence against them. But after reading the proclamation again, he ordered his militia to charge the mass of approximately a thousand protestors, which included women and children.

Captain Pouch's pouch could not protect the Diggers and Levellers on this day. Letters from the gentry indicated that forty to fifty rebels were killed and scores more captured and held in the Newton Church, which still stands today. The leaders, including Captain Pouch, were put to death and then quartered, a gruesome act that literally involved cutting the body into four parts to put on display. The remaining rebels were given the opportunity to apologize to the king and a document with over 100 signatures, many symbols used by those who were illiterate, is still held at Boughton House. When the authorities finally opened the magical pouch, they only found a small hunk of green, moldy cheese, or so the Chronicles state.

The Montagus, buttressed by the favor of the king, became one of the wealthiest families in England through vast enclosures of common lands. In 1628, Lord Montagu was given the patent and wardenship over Rockingham Forest, and the heirs of Boughton House, the Dukes of Buccleuch, amassed an enormous array of properties across Northamptonshire and in Scotland. By 1995, they had become the largest landowners in the United Kingdom, with holdings of 116,550 hectares (288,000 acres).[26]

In the centuries that followed, most of the remaining land in England was enclosed and transformed, from common areas for scavenging and animal husbandry to bounded properties owned by individuals. In the aftermath of a smaller 1517 revolt against enclosure during the reign of Henry VIII, Cardinal Thomas Wolsey had ordered an inquisition into the scale of enclosure and found that in most areas it represented only 0.5 percent of the land. The most enclosed counties in 1517 were Northamptonshire at 2.21 percent and Oxfordshire at 2.47 percent.[27] After the Midlands Revolt, another similar but smaller inquiry found that Northamptonshire was 4.3 percent enclosed by 1607. In spite of the protests by Captain Pouch and his rebels, by the end of the seventeenth century, 25 percent of all the land in England was enclosed.[28] In the eighteenth century, the government of the United Kingdom dropped its opposition to enclosures and established an official system to manage the process. Informal, private enclosures continued, but most major enclosures were done officially through the parliamentary enclosure system, which included provisions to ensure that small-scale tenants were compensated for their losses, though often with unproductive lands of a similar size.[29] Estimates by historians Michael Edward Turner and James Chapman suggest that an additional 25 to 30 percent of the entire land of England was formally enclosed in the eighteenth and nineteenth centuries through parliamentary enclosures.[30] In *The Making of the English Working Class*, which details the effects of enclosure as the process came to an end in the early nineteenth century, E. P. Thompson emphasizes that the process did not spread the wealth of property to all. It concentrated wealth in the hands of the elite. In the enclosure of Barton-on-Humber, he wrote, three people were granted more than 1,200 acres each, while fifty-one people were awarded between one and three acres.[31]

Small protests against enclosure persisted for centuries, but peasants never again rebelled in such large numbers as they did in the Midlands Revolt. As the whole of England became private property, laws were written to criminalize activities that were previously protected in the Magna Carta and the Charter of the Forest. Foraging, collecting estovers (firewood), and hunting in enclosed forests and fields were no longer common rights but were considered criminal theft that could land a peasant in jail.[32] If three or more people gathered and destroyed an enclosure, it was treated as a riot. If more than forty people gathered to protest at a field, it became treason.[33] Michael Hardt and Antonio Negri, authors of *Empire* and *Multitude*, argue that "law has always been a privileged domain for recognizing and establishing control over the common."[34] Property ownership also became a key marker of membership that perpetuated the exclusion of the poor, minorities, and women from other rights such as suffrage in early democracies.[35]

A similar process of enclosure occurred across most of Europe and North America in the nineteenth century. In the United States, the Homestead Acts divided the West into private property; the invention of barbed wire allowed huge claims to be cheaply and effectively enforced on a massive scale.[36] Europeans exported the idea of private property to their colonial holdings around the world by mapping, surveying, and dividing up the lands they controlled.[37] Throughout their conquered lands in Asia, Africa, and the Americas, they claimed land for the state, divided it up into private properties, and distributed it to colonists.

Globally, the enclosure of common lands into private property continues to the present day. Southeast Asia is one of the front lines. There are new rounds of enclosures as common jungles are mapped, surveyed, and enclosed into private property to sell to developers for oil and gas exploration or to convert to palm-oil plantations.[38] Furthermore, scholars argue that contemporary enclosure extends beyond simply land, and includes the privatization of public wealth, what geographer David Harvey calls "accumulation by dispossession."[39] "Whether in the form of resource wars, the often violent seizure of public lands for private capital, bio-piracy, the destruction of the global environmental commons, or the revanchist onslaught on public services across the Global North, capitalism is dependent on the division, conversion, and demolition of various forms of public life," write geographers Alex Jeffrey, Colin McFarlane, and Alex Vasudevan.[40]

Enclosures limited access to common forests and displaced the poor in rural England; contemporary resource enclosures in Asia and Africa are producing similar results. The enclosures restrict the movement of the poor into a forest, mining area, or fishery, but simultaneously force people to move when their livelihoods are cut off. From 2010 to 2015, development projects such as hydroelectric dams funded by the World Bank displaced 3.4 million people.[41] The result of these projects is that low-intensity traditional uses, like subsistence farming, are replaced by high-intensity extractions, like mines or industrial agriculture, that produce wealth for the landowners and tax revenues for the state at the expense of the former residents and of the environment. In the process, what had previously been land that anyone could access became bounded and enclosed property that belonged exclusively to someone.

The Peace of Westphalia

Eleven years after the Midlands Revolt, another revolt across Europe transformed how sovereignty and governance were organized by introducing a similar system of boundaries and enclosed territories at the level of the state. In 1618, when the first shots of what would be called the Thirty Years' War were fired, the territories of states and monarchies in Europe were not hard lines—and they were not derived from maps. In what are today Germany, Austria, and the Czech Republic, dozens of small and medium-sized city-states had different levels of control over their lands. Most were loosely under the authority of the Holy Roman Empire, but often the local lords had expansive control over the day-to-day affairs. The large kingdoms of France, Spain, and the Holy Roman Empire were not based on contiguous states with homogenous populations, either. Instead, diverse cultures and languages were joined by tribute or marriage. Their armies consisted of hired mercenaries who were not drawn from their own citizens (the etymology of the word soldier is from the Latin *soldarius*, "to fight for pay") and militias often had no real connection to the king or lord for whom they fought. They were not protecting their homeland or fighting in honor of their nation. Consequently, making war was often as much a business decision as a national sacrifice. It might bankrupt the realm, but often would not result in the deaths of many local boys. Indeed, on occasion, soldiers from the same place found themselves fighting against each after they were hired by distant adversaries.[42]

The Thirty Years' War (1618–1648) marked a moment of transition, when the older system of overlapping authority began to be replaced by modern sovereign states that claimed absolute authority over all the land, resources, and people in a territory based on borders drawn on a map. Just as new cartographic techniques allowed the estates of lords to be mapped and reimagined as bounded spaces, mapmaking transformed how states conceived of their land and their control over their realms.[43] The idea of borders as lines on maps began to replace the idea of frontiers of actual control on the ground. The names of some of the key players in the lead-up to the

Thirty Years' War—Bohemia, the Palatinate, Wittenberg, and Savoy—are unfamiliar to most people because they have since been incorporated into larger European states in the political transformations that followed.

The dispute that led to the war was about religion and was initiated by Martin Luther's Protestant Reformation. Luther was a professor of theology who became disenchanted with corruption in the Catholic Church, particularly the practice of paying indulgences to priests to atone for sins. He believed that God alone had the ability to grant forgiveness. In 1517 he wrote his *Ninety-Five Theses*, which in some accounts he nailed to the door of his local church in Wittenberg. The split between Catholic and Protestant versions of Christianity led to disputes over whether the local lord, a distant monarch, or the Pope had the authority to decide the religion of a town or region. The Peace of Augsburg, signed in 1555, was meant to resolve this by allowing local princes to determine the religion in their states, but it only temporarily settled the issue because it only applied to Lutheranism, not other new Protestant denominations such as Calvinism.

The crowning of Ferdinand II as the Holy Roman Emperor in 1619, at the beginning of the Thirty Years' War, set the stage for the long war that followed. Ferdinand had two passions that put him at odds with many of his restive subjects. First, he was a devout Catholic who lived a pious life. He attended mass daily and even engaged in self-abasement.[44] To him, Catholic religious beliefs were absolute; he worked to undo the accommodations and arrangements that his predecessors had made for Protestant lords and nobles. Second, he believed in the absolute authority of the monarch as the sovereign, which meant that any previous limits on the crown's authority were not legal, because they violated this sovereign authority from God. He worked to reestablish his prerogative and undermine other councils and rules that favored the wealthy elite in his realm.

Frederick V, the elector of Palatine, a small region in south-western Germany today but a semi-independent city-state in 1618, saw things differently. He was a Protestant who wanted to protect the rights of his townspeople to control their religious and economic decisions. In 1619, he was offered the crown of the king of Bohemia at the beginning of the Bohemian revolt against the imposition of Catholicism in the lands of the Holy Roman Empire. Frederick had developed ties to the other non-Catholic states, most notably England, and expected help in the looming fight against Ferdinand and the Holy Roman Empire. The help did not come. His forces were defeated within a year and he lived out the remainder of his short life in exile in the Dutch Republic. The early defeat did not end the revolt. A series of outside powers continued to be pulled into the fighting in central Europe as Denmark, France, Spain, and Sweden joined the war, which continued through the 1640s.

The Thirty Years' War devastated farmland, towns, and the population of central Europe. From 1631 to 1636 the city of Mainz "lost perhaps 25 percent of its dwellings, 40 percent of its population, and 60 percent of its wealth."[45] More people died, in proportion to the total population, than during World War II. By the 1640s, after almost thirty years of continuous war, there was still not a clear winner. Despite the devastation of central Europe, the disputes remained unresolved and the war dragged on.

The treaties that ended the war, collectively known as the Peace of Westphalia, represented a break with the past in several significant ways. Historian Peter Wilson writes that "Westphalia's significance lies not in the number of conflicts it tried to resolve, but in the methods and ideals it applied."[46] The resolution of the conflict set in motion the enclosure of the majority of the surface of the earth as state territories within borders.

The first significant result was that the treaties gave the

state authority over all political and economic decisions, while maintaining a space for the church in spiritual affairs only.[47] The agreement also weakened the authority of local lords by prohibiting small entities like estates from forming militias and sending envoys to foreign powers. It guaranteed princes "their ancient rights, prerogatives, freedoms, privileges, free exercise of territorial right, in ecclesiastic and territorial matters, in their domains, regalia, and possessions by virtue of this present Transaction: that they never can or ought to be removed by anyone under any pretext."[48] The Pope rejected the agreement, but his protests did not undermine it. The result is that power was devolved down from the Pope and the vast monarchies to middle-sized states, but also moved up from estates and small villages to the regional level. This consolidated and clarified authority and located it with the middle level of the state, reducing the influence of cities, empires, and the Pope.

The second consequence was the creation of a system of diplomacy through international agreement. It was the first significant meeting in which representatives from almost all of the European powers were participating in the same discussion. Wilson called it "the birth of the modern international order based on sovereign states."[49] Although there were many more wars in Europe, disputes became more frequently resolved at meetings over maps and less frequently on the battlefield. This ushered in the system of ambassadors and full-time representatives in the capitals of each state, a process that contributes to the symbolic recognition of the authority of each state within its territories.

The third consequence was the emergence of a system of borders to designate these new zones of territorial sovereignty. The agreement itself does not include maps and is not focused on the specifics of territorial boundaries, but it established the principal of territorial control and mutual recognition of authority. In the years after Westphalia, this system was tested out first by Sweden and Brandenburg when they divided Pomerania, a region on the southern Baltic coast in contemporary Germany and Poland, and laid out boundary stones in 1653.[50] More significantly, in the late 1650s, Spain and France met to establish a boundary in the Pyrenees between the two kingdoms, which resulted in the 1659 Treaty of the Pyrenees.[51] Prior to the agreement, most valleys in the mountains operated under local authority, but in the ensuing centuries the treaty oriented the people on each side of the border toward their new capital cities of Paris and Madrid. The resulting line on a map is still the boundary between the two states today. Nevertheless, France and Spain did not get around to marking the border on the ground with boundary stones until the Treaties of Bayonne in 1866 and 1868. The significance of the post-Westphalian era is that boundaries drawn on maps became the critical location for the division of the political space of the world.

After colonialism: Arbitrary borders and artificial states

The new system allowed each European state to consolidate power in its territory in ways that had not been possible when there were overlapping and contested claims to resources, people, and land.[52] Within their bounded territory, states could build roads to improve communication between the center and outlying areas. They could standardize the official language in government offices and schools and standardize measurements and land records to improve administration and tax collection. They could count the people and survey the land to allow for more efficient governance. Over time, the standardization of these practices within each state accentuated the similarities within each state and the differences between them. Over several hundred years, the states of Europe transitioned from a collection of loosely affiliated villages and cities that had relative autonomy into single political spaces with strong central governments marked by sharp boundaries.[53] There are many clear benefits to this system. States provided protection for their population in the form of police and judges. They developed infrastructure that facilitated movement and trade. Later, they began to provide aid to the population through unemployment payments, health care, and retirement pay.

As the post-Westphalian state system was institutionalized in Europe, many states used the growing wealth from tax collections to expand their territory in distant colonies. The colonies provided the European states with new lands to conquer, new resources to extract, and wealth to fuel the economies of the capital. When European colonists arrived in these places, they treated them as *terra nullius*, empty land that could be claimed and used by the Europeans. There were, of course, people already living in these places, but the lack of what the Europeans perceived as state structures meant that they could be conquered. They colonized the Americas, India, and other parts of Asia in the seventeenth and eighteenth centuries, removing local leaders, mapping the land, and creating European-style political systems.

Africa, on the whole, was colonized much later than other places. Only 10 percent of the continent was colonized in 1881. In what came to be known as the "scramble for Africa" or the "partition of Africa," multiple European states vied for control of resources and had overlapping spheres of influence in the 1880s. Following the precedent of Westphalia to work out territorial disputes through meetings and diplomacy, the European powers agreed to meet in Berlin in late 1884 to provide some order to the colonization of Africa. The conference was initiated by German chancellor Otto von Bismarck, and representatives met in a room with a huge map of Africa on the wall. After several months of discussion, they settled on zones of influence that effectively gave each European state the authority to colonize those areas. Belgium was awarded what is today the Congo. France maintained influence over North Africa as well as much of West Africa. Germany was awarded what is today Namibia and Tanzania. Portugal took Angola and Mozambique. The British maintained zones of influence across the continent, including present-day Egypt, Ghana, Kenya, Nigeria, South Africa, and Uganda.

Just as the partition of British India paid little attention to the linguistic, economic, or ethnic communities of South Asia, the boundaries established in Berlin did not consider local conditions such as tribal affiliations, language communities, or traditional economic networks. Lord Salisbury, the British prime minister, wrote in 1892, "[We] have been engaged in drawing lines upon maps where no white man's foot ever trod; we have been giving away mountains and rivers and lakes to each other, only hindered by the small impediment that we never knew exactly where the mountains and rivers and lakes were."[54] The agreements produced at the Berlin Conference regulated the colonization of Africa and established a framework that allowed European powers to replace local political systems with their own resource extraction regimes. By the beginning of World War I in 1914, 90 percent of the African continent had been colonized.

European colonies across Africa built railroad, road, and administrative networks that oriented their economies toward the coastlines, which allowed resources like rubber, timber, and copper to be transported away. Belgium, for example, was late to the practice of colonization but was able to secure control over a large section of Africa, what is today the Democratic Republic of the Congo. King Leopold II of Belgium established his own private state from 1885 until 1908, called the Congo Free State, which he ran as a brutal resource-extraction regime. It then became a Belgian colony until 1960. The interior regions of the Congo were still largely unvisited by Europeans; consequently, population estimates are difficult to make. Some estimates put the death toll of the first two decades of colonization at almost half the total population, or 8 to 10 million people. Joseph Conrad's *Heart of Darkness* (1899) dramatized the situation and Arthur Conan Doyle's *The Crime of the Congo* (1909) made the case for the violence and depravity of the colonization.

After World War II and the creation of the United Nations, European states were forced to begin the process of decolonization. In many of the colonies, there was no clear answer to what sort of political institution should come next. European colonizers had focused on resource extraction and had not invested in social infrastructure of schools, hospitals, or local industry. Moreover, the boundaries drawn in Berlin did not match the tribal, linguistic, or ethnic affiliations of the people. While there are fifty-four countries in Africa, more than 1,500 are languages spoken.[55] Some African leaders proposed a united single country of Africa after decolonization, but the easiest path was to maintain the artificial European boundaries from the Berlin Conference as the borders of the newly independent states, which allowed the colonial infrastructure to become the institutions of the state. Maintaining the colonial borders did not address the issues of diverse ethnic, tribal, or linguistic groups within a particular state or groups whose members straddle the borders of multiple states. In the former Belgian Congo, for example, the country's 60 million inhabitants are estimated to include 250 ethnic groups and speak 700 languages. In newly independent countries across Africa, people who spoke different languages, were members of different tribes, and were classified as different ethnicities suddenly found themselves officially a single "nation." In many cases, leaders favored people from their own groups, which resulted in autonomy and independence movements led by those outside the leader's group.

In 2016, there are approximately fifty active independence movements in Africa currently attempting to redraw national boundaries on the political map. Africa also has several failed states: countries that exist on the map and are recognized at the United Nations but do not have real control over much of their territory. In the past, if a state collapsed, a neighboring army would move in and take the land. However, after the creation of the UN, which protects the borders and sovereignty of all its member states, it is very difficult to change established borders. The result is a state like Somalia, which continues to appear on maps as a single country even though it has not had a functioning central government since 1991. Within the borders of Somalia there are two other unrecognized states, Somaliland and Puntland, that have autonomous control over about one-third of the former country of Somalia each. In the remaining third, militias and the Islamist group Al-Shabaab vie for what remains of the state. The internal conflicts, the lack of economic development, and the difficulty of acquiring a quality education are key factors in driving many migrants to leave their homes in these artificial African states and look for better opportunities elsewhere.

The first half of the twentieth century was also when borders were created throughout the rest of the colonial world. In the Middle East, the key period was the end of World War I as Britain, France, Russia, and local Arab leaders vied to shape the breakup of the Ottoman Empire in a way that suited their interests. Britain and France secretly agreed to separate areas of influence in the often derided Sykes–Picot Agreement of 1916, made between emissaries of the British and French governments. Although the Sykes–Picot maps do not match the current borders of Iraq, Syria, and Jordan in the Middle East, the agreement is often used as a stand-in to symbolize the fact that most of the borders were imposed by European powers and are not based on historical political or cultural divisions.[56] T. E. Lawrence, the British military officer depicted in the film *Lawrence of Arabia*, had promised Arab militias that if they rebelled against the Ottomans, Britain would support their independence, but the Sykes–Picot Agreement did not include any Arab states. The legacy of Sykes–Picot, along with the Paris Peace Conference of 1919, the San Remo Resolution of 1920, and the Cairo Conference of 1921, shaped the boundaries of the European Mandate territories in the Middle East that became independent countries in the 1930s and 1940s. Similar to Africa, the boundaries of the contemporary states of the Middle East do not match historical political entities or the ethnic makeup of the population on the ground. The state of Iraq consists of three distinct regions with different religious, ethnic, and cultural groups in the Kurdish north, the Sunni Arab center, and Shi'a Arab south. Syria has multiple distinct linguistic and ethnic groups within its state boundaries. Both states were held together for several decades through strong central governments, but once those were destabilized by the US invasion of Iraq in 2003 and the Arab Spring protests in 2011 in Syria, the states collapsed into internal conflict. In 2014, as the Islamic State announced the reformation of the Caliphate, it also highlighted its removal of the Syria–Iraq border as a triumph over Sykes–Picot and European imposed boundaries.[57]

The legacy of these European colonial boundaries in the Middle East is similar to that in Africa and India: conflict over artificial borders sends millions of migrants fleeing in search of better opportunities elsewhere. The maps on which these divisions are drawn do not simply represent a pre-existing reality, even as the placement and visualization of the natural world of rivers, mountains, and islands alongside the system of borders, states, and nations makes them appear just as natural. The very oldest boundary maps in Europe date from the 1650s, but even some of those were not marked on the ground until the 1800s. Most other borders are much newer inventions. All of them are artificial lines drawn on maps to exclude other people from access to resources and the right to move.

The enclosure of the ocean

At the turn of the twentieth century, the oceans were one of the last bastions of free movement and unclaimed resources on earth. Through the end of World War II, most states only claimed territorial seas stretching three nautical miles off their coasts. These zones were based on the "cannon-shot rule," corresponding to the area that could be defended by armaments on shore in the seventeenth century. Beyond that zone, more than 95 percent of the surface area of the oceans and 70 percent of the surface of the earth was open to fishing and free movement by any ships. However, in the twentieth century, states around the world aggressively expanded their control of ocean spaces in order to claim the resources and wealth that lay beneath the seafloor.[58]

Humans have used the seas for fishing and movement for millennia. The Polynesians traveled throughout the Pacific Ocean using the stars to navigate.[59] The Indian Ocean has a rich history of trade between Africa and South Asia.[60] The Mediterranean served as the transportation link for the Greek, Roman, and Phoenician civilizations.[61] During the period of European colonization, the high seas were important spaces for the transportation of goods around the world and for the control of distant lands. In the sixteenth century, as more vessels were making long-distance voyages, England, the Netherlands, Portugal, and Spain challenged each other for the ability to control the seas. The key positions on the right of free movement on the high seas were laid out by jurists in the Netherlands and England. Hugo Grotius, an influential Dutch jurist who also wrote significant texts about private property, made the case for the Dutch position in his *Mare Liberum* (1609), which argued that the seas are a common space for the shared use of all states for trading purposes. The English monarchy did not accept this position, primarily because they wanted to control fishing grounds near their coasts, which were being used at the time by boats from the Netherlands as well as Scandinavia. English legal scholar John Selden's *Mare Clausum* (1635) was a rejoinder to Grotius and argued that states could effectively treat coastal seas as their territories. By the early eighteenth century, the profits from long-distance trade outweighed the need for exclusive fishing grounds. All of the European powers accepted the notion of free movement on the high seas, with a limited three nautical miles off the coast as the territorial sea of a state.

This general agreement of three nautical miles held until the end of World War II. The realization that there were many resources in the ocean and under the seafloor that could be made productive with new extraction technologies has driven the changing political geography of the ocean.[62] In addition to fisheries, the demand for fossil fuels transformed states' claims to resources in the oceans as massive oil and gas reserves were discovered under coastal waters and on continental shelves. The United States was the first to challenge the status quo of freedom of movement on the high seas. In 1945, US president Harry Truman signed a proclamation that extended US claims to resources on all of its continental shelves "beneath the high seas but contiguous to the coasts of the United States."[63] The decision allowed a number of other countries to make similar claims to coastal resources as the traditional three-nautical-mile agreement collapsed. In the 1952 Santiago Declaration, Chile, Ecuador, and Peru declared 200 nautical mile zones to prevent fleets from Europe and North America from fishing in waters off their coasts.[64] By the late 1950s, it was clear that a new global agreement was needed to adjudicate these claims and to establish a global system for the governance of the high seas.[65]

This task was taken up by the United Nations, which held multiple conferences and produced interim agreements that settled some of the various issues. The final agreement was reached during the third UN Conference on the Law of the

Sea, which ran from 1973 to 1982. The conference produced the Law of the Sea (LOS) Convention in 1982, which came into force in 1994 after it was ratified by sixty member states. In 2016, 166 countries were parties to the LOS. The United States is not a signatory because it does not accept provisions about the deep seabed that restrict commercial extraction of resources, but it does follow all of the other provisions of the LOS that expanded the area of sovereign state control over resources.

The LOS encloses all of the oceans and transforms the open ocean into administered space, but divides it into several separate zones with different levels of control. The LOS retains the concept of territorial waters for all coastal states, but expands it from three to twelve nautical miles. In these areas the states have complete control over the laws, the resources, and the movement of ships. In order to allow states to extract resources from the ocean floor, the LOS agreement created exclusive economic zones (EEZs) that range from 12 to 200 nautical miles off the coast.[66] In EEZs there is free movement for ships on the surface, but the coastal states have control over all of the resources below the waterline, including fisheries, seafloor minerals, and fossil fuels under the seafloor bottom. Beyond the 200-nautical-mile EEZ, if the shallow continental shelf continues and does not impede on other states' EEZs, states can claim rights to the extended continental shelf, up to 350 nautical miles from the coast. In this zone, the surface is a space of free movement and the water column is open to fishing by any ships, but the coastal state has exclusive rights to exploit underground resources through oil and gas exploration. The remaining 55 percent of the oceans, which is called the deep seabed or the Area, is nominally still the high seas, with movement and fishing open to any ships. The deep seafloor is regulated by the International Seabed Authority, which is authorized to award exploration and mining contracts to extract minerals on the bottom. There are currently eight contractors exploring sites for future mining operations.[67]

In total, the Law of the Sea encloses over 40 percent of the world's common oceans and gives individual states the right to manage the resources there, often through contracts with corporations. Furthermore, even in the high seas, which are ostensibly a space of free movement, these rights are circumscribed by the requirement that all ships be flagged by a recognized state: "The high seas are open to all states, whether coastal or landlocked." Generally ships can move freely but there are a few very specific situations in which a military ship may interdict another ship on the high seas. Along with piracy and slave trading, the other two offenses are unauthorized broadcasting and not having a nationality. In legal terms, the high seas are a space for free movement for ships affiliated with states, not for all. In practice, the high seas are still a lawless place where ships change flags regularly, illegal fishing is rampant, and crimes are difficult to prosecute. Nevertheless, states claim these spaces and can move to institute control if necessary. This process is similar to territorial claims in past centuries—think of the westward expansion of the United States—which were often first made in theory on a map and not enacted on the ground for many decades or even centuries.

The race to occupy the zones of the ocean that were enclosed through the LOS continues, as coastal states map the seafloor bottom and claim resources under the extended continental shelf provision. In many places, because these zones are so far from the states' coastlines, they overlap with other states' claims. The Arctic Ocean is one of these resource frontiers where climate change has opened up access to seas that were previously inaccessible due to ice.[68] These new surveys have determined that there are large oil and gas reserves there, with the United States Geological Survey estimating that over 20 percent of the undiscovered and recoverable global reserves are north of the Arctic Circle.[69] In response, Canada,

Denmark, Norway, Russia, and the United States have rushed to establish their claims. In 2007, a Russian submarine planted a Russian flag on the seafloor bottom at the North Pole at a depth of 4,200 meters (14,000 feet). In response, Canada and Denmark have also claimed the North Pole and are requesting arbitration.

Bordered space

Enclosures of land, territory, and the oceans allow states to establish a legal means for controlling resources and excluding others from these spaces, with the LOS claiming more than one-third of the area of the world in a single political agreement. The unadministered spaces and peripheries that characterized the past were reorganized into a global system of territorial and resource control. Today almost all of the land in the world is claimed by states that possess the authority to use its resources and limit the movement of people. The boundaries that enclosed land into private property and established state sovereignty within territories and seas are treated as if they have always existed eternally, but even the oldest political borders are only a few hundred years old; most are only a few decades old. They are not the result of a transparent sorting of historical peoples into their own territories. Instead, borders are an efficient system for maintaining political control of an area through agreements and documents that are backed up with the threat of violence.

Although direct violence was used to impose these regulations, as the deaths at the end of the Midlands Revolt attest, these enclosures are more clearly examples of the structural violence of borders. They changed the relationship between people and the environment by redefining land and oceans as closed areas of ownership that can be exploited for economic gain, not common spaces to be shared and conserved. As individuals, corporations, and states gained ownership over land, the ability to make decisions on how to use the land shifted from a public to a private concern.

The current violence at borders that targets migrants fleeing war and economic inequality in search of a better life is the latest stage in the long-term conflict between states and rulers—who control land and want to protect their rights to the wealth and opportunity captured there—and people who move in order to gain new opportunities or leave repressive conditions. The enclosure of common lands and the lack of coherence within many decolonized states often result in violence and war as control over the mechanisms of power are contested, as is currently occurring in Syria, Iraq, Afghanistan, Somalia, and South Sudan. The irony is that migrants from these disorderly artificial states, which are the remnants of European colonialism, are denied the right to move to Europe to escape the artificial boundaries Europe left behind.

Chapter 6

Bounding Wages, Goods, and Workers

The collapse of the Rana Plaza building in Savar, Bangladesh, on April 24, 2013, killed 1,127 people and injured more than 2,500 more. Prior to the tragedy, Savar, a city of 1 million people on the outskirts of Dhaka, was primarily known as the location for the National Martyrs' Monument, which recognizes Bangladeshis who lost their lives during the independence movement. In recent years, the city had also become a key site for another revolution in Bangladesh: the emergence of the textile industry. At the time of the accident in 2013, the industry directly employed 4 million people and accounted for almost 80 percent of Bangladesh's exports. Savar was a popular location for textile factories because it was near the Dhaka airport, on the northern fringes of the city but outside the densely packed and overbuilt capital.

The Rana Plaza, as with many buildings in Bangladesh, was built over several years, with additional floors added to the construction beyond the original plans and without securing the proper permits. The building contained several garment factories that did contract work for a wide range of American and European retailers including Benetton, the Children's Place, Mango, and Walmart. On the day before the collapse, a government inspector ordered the building closed after large cracks appeared in the walls and foundation.[1] On the day of the collapse, the managers of several textile factories in the building assured workers everything was fine and ordered them to continue to work. After a power failure, a generator was turned on to allow production to continue, which shook the building enough to bring it down. The unimaginable death toll raised global awareness of working conditions in factories in Bangladesh and around the world.[2] In the aftermath, Mushamat Sokina Begum, a twenty-seven-year-old survivor who said she was paid about $50 per month, explained to Der Spiegel what it was like to work there: "We only get money if we're at the factory. There's no paid vacation. We sometimes work until 11 pm, always under pressure, always being told we should work faster so the orders are finished on time."[3]

A century earlier, in 1906, Upton Sinclair described similar conditions in meatpacking plants in Chicago in his fictionalized exposé The Jungle. The novel follows Jurgis, who is trying to make a life in Chicago but finds himself cast off by factory after factory. He continues to look for work and has to take some of the worst on offer. "Few visitors ever saw them, and the few who did would come out looking like Dante," wrote Sinclair of the fertilizer-works section of a plant where Jurgis worked. Anyone entering, he continued, would "begin to cough and choke; and then, if he were still obstinate, he would find his head beginning to ring, and his veins in his forehead throb, until finally he would be assailed by an overpowering blast of ammonia fumes, and would turn and run for his life, and come out half-dazed."[4]

The book shocked the public with its unflinching portrayal of dangerous, horrid working conditions and the unsanitary and grotesque process through which food was produced. Its most immediate impact was on food safety: several significant laws regulating meatpacking and food purity were passed in 1906.[5] It would be another thirty years before there were basic standards that regulated working conditions in factories across all sectors of the US economy. In the 1910s and 1920s, there was still a lot of money to be made in these factories, but eventually the slave-like work conditions and low wages contributed to the economic collapse of the 1930s.

Just as there are similarities in the working conditions in factories from the early twentieth century in the United States and in countries like Bangladesh today, there are also similarities in the economic crashes that occurred at the end of these economic cycles: both the great recession of the 2000s and the Great Depression of the 1930s occurred after a period of sustained economic growth with light regulations.[6] The growth produced enormous profits for companies, which drove stock markets to new heights. Both situations turned out to be unsustainable, with income disparities widening as little of the new wealth trickled down to the workers. Without consumers to buy the new products, they produced long and deep economic recessions with a painful long-term period of unemployment. After the collapses, the United States elected populist Democratic presidents who attempted to put in place more regulations and spent government money to stimulate the economy.

Scholars often look for solutions to current problems in the contrasting economic theories of John Maynard Keynes and Friedrich Hayek, which were formulated during the Great Depression. Keynesians argue that the depression of the 1930s and the recession of the 2000s were the result of the over-extension of capitalism in an underregulated market.[7] The solution, for them, is more regulations to provide a check on unbridled capitalism and an increase in government spending, in order to pump liquidity back into the markets and keep workers employed. Free market economists of the Chicago School argue that markets will correct themselves, á la Adam Smith's invisible hand.[8] These scholars agree that capitalism was overextended prior to both crises, but suggest that the overextension occurred due to government interference, which created an imbalance and encouraged unsound business decisions. However, there is a major difference between the two downturns which both schools ignore: In the intervening seventy years, borders have hardened to prevent the movement of workers and create piecemeal national regulations that corporations can manipulate. Jurisdictional differences and movement restrictions at borders will make it much harder to improve the conditions in factories in Bangladesh than it was to improve the conditions in the Chicago meatpacking industry a century ago.

From the Gilded Age to globalization

The period from the 1890s through the 1920s was the first golden age of capitalism. Industrialists utilized new technologies and the growing population of unemployed workers in US and European cities. These people provided cheap labor for the factories, mines, and warehouses driving the emerging industrial economy. On the one hand, the availability of any job was welcomed because the only other option was often scrounging on the streets. On the other hand, this sector of the economy was completely new and was not regulated by the government. Because there seemed to be an endless supply of available workers, these new factories and mines often paid miniscule wages, offered dirty and dangerous jobs, and required long, grueling hours like those described in *The Jungle*. There was no impetus for bosses to treat their workers better, as labor was abundant and workers easily replaceable.

However, the low wages meant that few workers could afford the goods and services they made, which led to factory closures, while the dull and demeaning working conditions meant that worker productivity was low and workers frequently left seeking better opportunities elsewhere. The small elite who could afford these goods were eventually hampered by debt, and the system could not sustain itself. Meanwhile, during the boom years, the wealth gap between the rich and the poor grew dramatically. Thomas Piketty, author of *Capital in the Twenty-First Century*, showed that inequality reached its peak in 1929 in the United States, just before the crash that preceded the Great Depression.[9]

The origins of the 1929 crash and the Great Depression can be traced to World War I.[10] Prior to the war there was a relatively free market between the United States, Europe, and South America, the main participants in the global economy. Migrants moved freely to new settler colonies and traded goods. In the aftermath of World War I, many European countries were in extreme debt to the United States, which began to institute more restrictions on movement at borders. It did this with immigration quotas, such as the Immigration Act of 1924, which limited Asian and Southern European migrants, as well as tariffs to protect American agriculture and industry. This undermined the economies of European countries, who relied on US consumers to buy their goods and generate revenue to pay back their debts to the United States. Instead, they began to default on their loans. Meanwhile, within the United States, the optimism of the 1920s was leading many Americans to begin to purchase new consumer goods on credit. By the late 1920s, these debts had grown and consumers could not continue to drive the US economy.

Then the stock market crashed in 1929, wiping out one-third of the value of the market, though this only affected the rich who were invested in it. The drop itself was not the problem, but it was a catastrophic blow to the confidence of consumers, with newspapers treating it as a barometer of the health of the economy. Consumers stopped taking out loans and delayed purchases, which began a downward spiral of unemployment as companies could not pay salaries to workers.[11] Those unemployed workers in turn bought even less, which resulted in more layoffs and cutbacks at factories.

President Herbert Hoover did not believe in government intervention in the economy. He refused to make direct payments to the unemployed and he allowed banks to fail, thinking it was a normal part of the economic correction.

During his four years in office, 20 percent of banks collapsed, which further eroded the confidence of consumers; by the time he set up a banking support system, it was too late. It is estimated that 25 percent of American workers were unemployed in 1932. Franklin Delano Roosevelt rode this discontent into the presidency (1933–1945).

Despite heavy resistance, Roosevelt and his allies were able to enact the legislation that came to be known as the New Deal: the Banking Act of 1933, often referred to as Glass–Steagall after its primary congressional sponsors, and the Fair Labor Standards Act. These regulations prevented excess speculation by business, included stimulus spending in the form of massive public-works projects, and protected workers by establishing a minimum wage and a forty-hour work week and banning child labor.[12] This was possible because the companies, the banks, the workers, and the consumers were all within the United States. According to the political theorist Isaiah Berlin, Roosevelt's "great social experiment was conducted with an isolationist disregard for the outside world."[13]

The debate continues between Keynesian and Chicago School economists about whether the Great Depression ended because of these laws or in spite of them, since there was no pure test of their effectiveness after the US and global economies were disrupted by World War II. In the United States, the war provided a huge government stimulus in which an enormous amount of money was spent building weapons and conducting the war. At its conclusion, more money was needed for reconstruction. Not insignificantly, the war created a new sense of optimism in the United States as the blues of the Depression era were replaced with the feeling that the United States was a force for good in the world that had stood up against evil and defeated it.

In the thirty-year period after World War II, the US economy grew expansively. From 1945 until 1975, real wages almost tripled; income inequality reached its lowest point in 1972.

Economic growth was fueled by government spending programs. The GI Bill educated returning soldiers and funded research at universities, which gave US companies an educated workforce and new technologies. The Highway and Transportation Funding Act funded construction companies, provided jobs, and established the necessary infrastructure for more cars and long-distance trucking.[14] This made it easier for companies to sell products. The New Deal regulations also created favorable conditions for workers. Minimum-wage laws established reasonable salaries for workers across all industries, and because all US companies had to comply with them, everyone was on equal footing. The forty-hour work week created weekends, a novel idea that gave workers the time to pursue leisure activities. With their higher wages, they could buy new products to use in their free time. The emerging middle class used its growing wealth to buy homes in the suburbs, which funded the construction industry. The suburbs were often far from factories, so workers had to buy new cars to drive to work, which contributed to road building and the auto industry. They had to fill their new homes with consumer goods, which spurred the manufacturing sector. In turn, all of these purchases created more jobs, which generate more wealth and propelled more people into the middle class.

Labor unions played an important role in this economy. The unions guaranteed a stable, dependable, and skilled labor force. In return, they demanded high wages, benefits, and long-term contracts. With government support via regulations, the unions helped to create extremely favorable conditions for workers across a wide range of industries. This system worked because all US companies were in similar circumstances; none was able to undercut the others by paying low wages. Instead, they outcompeted each other by having dedicated, skilled workers who were extremely productive and made high-quality products.

The United States operated as an effectively closed system in which the corporations, workers, regulators, and consumers were all in the same bounded regulatory space.[15] Borders were key. There were always goods and services from other countries in the American marketplace, but the driving force was domestic production and consumption. Even Hayek recognized in *The Road to Serfdom* that some regulations are acceptable as long as they apply equally to everyone, "so long as these restrictions affect all potential producers equally and are not used as an indirect way of controlling prices and quantities. To prohibit the use of certain poisonous substances, or to require special precautions in their use, to limit working hours or to require certain sanitary arrangements, is fully compatible with the preservation of competition."[16] This might not have made for the most efficient model, because regulations artificially inflated wages and the prices of products. But as long as US companies were playing by the same rules for wages, working conditions, and environmental controls, minimum standards could be maintained and the companies could be successful. US corporations were insulated by the country's physical isolation and the logistical difficulties of transporting goods from abroad. American consumers were satisfied with the quality of American-made products. Through 1970, imports and exports accounted for only 5 percent of the gross domestic product (GDP) of the United States.[17]

The transition from a bounded national to a globalized economy began in the 1970s and has been variously described as a transition from a Fordist to a post-Fordist economy, from a mass-production to a flexible-accumulation economy, and from a modern to a postmodern economy.[18] All of these labels denote a similar shift away from an economy defined by large factories in wealthy economies that employed unionized workers, under regulation by their national governments, and predominantly produced goods for domestic consumers. This older economic model has been replaced by a globalized economy in which multinational corporations establish factories in the cheapest place possible and then ship those goods over long distances and across borders. The hardening of borders was critical to this change, defining the edges of different regulatory spaces and limiting the movement of labor. These combined to create pools of low-wage workers in areas with minimal environmental and labor regulations.

This transition was driven by technological changes and new modes of production. New container ships could carry enormous loads, which reduced transportation costs by virtue of their sheer volume. The expansion of telephone and, later, computer technologies allowed better communication between distant offices. Additionally, new production methods reduced costs for corporations abroad.[19] These included high-tech factories that replaced expensive and inflexible workers with cheaper and more versatile computers and automated machinery. It also meant relying on shorter contracts with nonunion labor forces. These workers were easier to lay off and were paid less. A smaller, nonunionized workforce benefits corporations by allowing them to adapt to new market conditions quickly by ramping up production when there is demand, stopping production when there is a decline, and changing products when consumers want something different. Flexibility and efficiency, rather than quality and reliability, became dominant.

Many US companies did not make these changes in the 1970s because of government restrictions, while the older production model of the 1950s remained profitable. The auto industry is a good example. In 1965, 90 percent of the cars sold in the United States were US-made. Japanese car brands like Toyota suddenly became more desirable after the 1973 oil crisis. The crisis was precipitated by an oil embargo by the Organization for Petroleum-Exporting Countries that targeted the United States, Japan, and many European countries that supported Israel in the 1973 Yom Kippur War. As gas prices increased dramatically, the smaller and more fuel-efficient Toyota vehicles began to cut into the sales of American cars. In 1970, fewer than 400,000 Japanese cars were sold in the United States; in 1980, it was 1.8 million, and more than 25 percent of the cars sold were made outside of the United States. In 2009 it was 56 percent. Each of these foreign sales represented fewer domestic sales.[20]

Similar transitions occurred across the economy as the free trade of globalization replaced the closed domestic market. While, in 1970, imports only accounted for 5 percent of GDP, the percentage had doubled to 10 percent by 1980; by 2000, import goods accounted for 15 percent of GDP.[21] Global trade tripled from 1998 to 2008, from $5.5 trillion to $16 trillion.[22] As US consumers increasingly turned to goods produced in foreign countries by foreign workers, demand for US goods dropped, factories closed, and workers were laid off. This meant less money for consumption, which meant less production.[23] The cycle of mass production and mass consumption continued, but in reverse.

Corporations and borders

By the 1980s, the even playing field that US companies had enjoyed for decades had disappeared, with many foreign companies operating under lax wage, labor, and environmental regulations. This was fundamentally a problem of borders. Because each state is guaranteed sovereignty over economic and environmental decisions, borders become lines of distinction between different systems. Inevitably, some of these systems will favor workers more than others, some will protect the environment more than others, and some will benefit corporations by providing a space of minimal interference in the accumulation of wealth. US companies were often demonized for changing their models, but they faced two choices: go out of business or close their US factories and move to locations with cheaper labor. Most chose the latter.

As manufacturing jobs left the United States and Europe through outsourcing, corporations were able to get the same work done at a fraction of the cost. It hurt workers in the United States, but was great for corporations. It drove up the overall GDP. Financial centers such as New York benefited because the headquarters of corporations supported a range of industries that facilitated global trade, such as law firms, banks, and insurance companies. These high-wage industries supported service industries in these cities, including hotels, restaurants, and high-end retail. But for the emergent middle class of the postwar era, globalization was disastrous. As manufacturing jobs moved overseas (the manufacturing industry shrank from almost 30 percent of US jobs in 1970 to 8 percent in 2012[24]), many of the victories unions had won— high wages, substantial pensions, health care benefits—were lost. The workers who remain in the United States today are paid far less than unionized workers were a generation ago. Between 1973 and 2013, real wages (when standardized to remove the effect of inflation) increased by only 14 percent, from $48,741 to $55,740. Recall that from 1945 to 1973 they increased almost 300 percent. On a longer term and a broader scale, the low wages in the factories failed to create a new consumer market for goods and services.

Several institutions and global agreements facilitated the globalization of manufacturing and trade. The World Trade Organization (WTO) functions to remove trade barriers between countries in order to allow free trade. The WTO came into being in 1994 and replaced the previous General Agreement on Tariffs and Trade (GATT), an agreement from the late 1940s that established trade rules between countries in the aftermath of World War II. The basic idea is that all WTO member countries have to be consistent in their trade agreements with all other members, not creating special arrangements for some countries. The WTO promotes reciprocity between states so that they give each other the same levels of access, much as Hayek sought. Finally, it provides a venue for states to bring complaints against the practices of other member states.

Free-trade agreements between individual countries follow the broad goals of the WTO by establishing wide-ranging open markets. NAFTA established common markets in Canada, Mexico, and the United States when it came into effect in 1994, although some provisions were not phased in until as late as 2008. The agreement removed tariffs on many goods, with a particular focus on agriculture and textiles, but did not allow the free movement of people. Assessing its impact is difficult because it is challenging to separate out the impact of NAFTA from economic trends or trade with other places, China specifically.[25] Nevertheless, there is broad agreement that NAFTA increased the volume of trade between the three states and influenced companies' decisions to move factories out of the United States and into Mexico. A 2011 study found that 682,900 US jobs had moved to Mexico.[26] The Congressional Budget Office concluded that some of this may have occurred anyway due to the underlying differences in wages and regulations between Mexico and the United States. The overall impact on exports and imports was "small" and increased GDP "slightly."[27]

The latest example of a free trade agreement is the Trans-Pacific Partnership (TPP), which was signed in 2016 between the United States, Australia, Brunei, Canada, Chile, Japan, Malaysia, Mexico, New Zealand, Peru, Singapore, and Vietnam, which, combined, account for 40 percent of the world's trade. China is not currently part of the agreement, but is observing and may join later. The broad outlines of the agreement attempt to remove trade restrictions between states to allow corporations to access more markets throughout the Pacific, without easing restrictions on the movement of workers. Supporters argue that free trade lifts everyone and that if the United States does not make the agreement now, then China will replace it as a global economic superpower. Critics of the deal argue that it will further erode workers' rights in the United States, while not providing protections for workers elsewhere.

The most controversial provisions of the TPP agreement are clauses that give corporations the ability to sue national governments if they impose limits on trade that run contrary to the agreement. The problem with these provisions is that they shift the sovereign authority of independent states over to corporations. The TPP has an Investor-State Dispute Settlement provision, common in many trade agreements. In the past, these clauses were used to create a tribunal composed of lawyers to decide if the state had unfairly canceled a contract.[28] Although these provisions have existed since 1959, they were not used regularly until the 1990s, when there were less than ten per year. In 2012 and 2013, there were more than fifty claims each year.[29] One of the largest disputes, for $1.4 billion, was brought by the Swedish firm Vattenfall after Germany canceled plans to build nuclear power plants in the aftermath of the Fukushima disaster in Japan. In the TPP the clause is expanded to allow investors to sue if the actions of the state affect their expected ability to make a profit. Consequently, almost any regulation that limits a corporation can be contested, including environmental regulations, minimum wages, and laws that establish basic working conditions.[30] The Transatlantic Trade and Investment Partnership, under negotiation between the European Union and the United States, has a similar investor-dispute clause.[31] Although trade agreements continue to be popular among governments and corporations, a 2015 report by the Center for Economic and Policy Research found that free trade agreements accounted for growth of only 0.014 percent, or forty-three cents per person, in the United States.[32]

Just as US companies in the first decade of the twentieth century used cheap, widely available labor and unregulated labor markets to make enormous profits domestically, corporations now use cheap, widely available labor and unregulated labor markets to make enormous profits globally. Boundaries create discontinuities that can be exploited, and corporations use the multiple labor pools to increase profits.[33] But while global institutions like the WTO and free trade agreements allow corporations to operate across borders, regulators and workers are contained by them.

Borders capture labor

The movement of factory work out of the United States and into poor and decolonized countries has had uneven effects on those countries' economies. China's size and enormous population have allowed it to extract some concessions from corporations in order to build its technological and economic infrastructure. Since China's wages and costs have gone up, many corporations are increasingly looking to other options with even lower wages and fewer environmental regulations. Bangladesh, with its enormous population and very low wages, has filled this niche.

Since Bangladesh gained its independence from Pakistan in 1971, its population has grown from 67 million to 160 million in 2015. Along with the transition to an independent economy, this has forced millions to leave rural areas to look for better opportunities.[34] Most people in rural Bangladesh work in small-scale agriculture or in tiny workshops that fix shoes, repair bicycles, weave mats, or sell tea for the equivalent of one US dollar or less per day.[35] The lack of industry and opportunity in rural areas drives many to head to the closest major cities, Dhaka or Chittagong. The population of Dhaka in 1951 was 336,000; by 2013 it was estimated to be

15 million, and it continues to grow at 4.2 percent per year. As in other countries across the decolonized world, Bangladesh was desperate for jobs but lacked local industries after two centuries of British colonization.[36]

With raw materials and finished goods that are lightweight and easy to transport over long distances, textile jobs shifted to lower-wage countries like China, Pakistan, and Bangladesh. In the 1950s almost all clothing sold in the United States was US-made, but today it is less than 2 percent.[37] The garment sector in Bangladesh has grown rapidly in the past twenty-five years. China, with a population almost ten times as large as Bangladesh, is the only country with a larger garment-export sector. In 2013, almost 6 percent of clothes sold in the United States were from Bangladesh, a total of almost $5 billion worth of imported textiles.[38]

The Bangladesh Garment Manufacturers and Exporters Association (BGMEA), an industry organization, reports that there were only 384 garment factories in Bangladesh in 1984; that number had grown to over 5,600 in 2013.[39] BGMEA estimates that the sector indirectly employs 20 million people. In 2013, garment exports totaled $24 billion, which accounted for 77 percent of the total exports of the country. The next largest sectors are jute and jute products at 5 percent and frozen foods at 2.7 percent.[40] The industry group's website emphasizes the advantages of Bangladesh over China, including the growth of wages in China and the large low-wage labor force in Bangladesh.[41] The main message is that Bangladesh is the cheapest option and suppliers should consider moving factories from China to Bangladesh. However, being the cheapest and least regulated comes at a cost.

In 2013, when the Rana Plaza collapsed, the minimum wage in Bangladesh was $39 per month, one of the lowest in the world. If a worker worked a standard eight-hour shift five days per week, that wage would be twenty-four cents per hour. Many workers work many more hours than that per month because they are routinely given productivity targets that are impossible to meet. In order to finish the task, workers have to stay late or work on holidays or days off.[42] If they miss their targets they are not paid or are fired.

In the aftermath of the Rana Plaza collapse, the largest disaster in a string of other fires and collapses in the past five years in Bangladesh, there was substantial pressure on the government and international retailers to improve the physical infrastructure of factories to prevent fires and building collapses. Many large European retailers signed the Accord on Fire and Building Safety in Bangladesh, while American companies including Gap and Walmart created the Alliance for Bangladesh Worker Safety.[43] The government raised the minimum wage in Bangladesh from $39 to $68 per month in December 2013.[44] Human Rights Watch argues that focusing on the safety of structures and factory fire policies deflects attention away from working conditions and hours: "In many cases these remain dire, in breach both of national law and the standards that are often stipulated by the Western retailers who buy most of Bangladesh's garments."[45]

According to the Human Rights Watch report, which was based on interviews with workers at factories in and around Dhaka, common complaints about the operation of factories included that factories paid late, underpaid, and failed to provide vacation or maternity leave and bonuses guaranteed by law. Most workers faced pressure to be highly productive, with verbal and physical abuse for underproduction; were discouraged from taking bathroom breaks; and were forced to work overtime to meet unrealistic targets. Although the right to form unions is guaranteed by the constitution of Bangladesh, unions are routinely busted by employers, who intimidate organizers with verbal and physical violence.[46] In 2015, there were unions in less than 10 percent of Bangladeshi factories, despite an increase since Rana Plaza. Furthermore, unions are banned in Bangladesh's export processing zones, special areas set up specifically to house new factories and to create as favorable a business environment as possible.[47] The report is very blunt: "Factory owners want to maximize profits, so they will cut corners on safety issues, on ventilation, and on sanitation. They will not pay overtime or offer assistance in case of injuries. They will not build fire exits or stock fire extinguishers. Many of them treat their workers like slaves."[48]

The government of Bangladesh has little leverage because the revenue of many of the largest corporations is larger than the GDP of the entire country. For example, Walmart's revenues in 2012 would make it the twentieth-largest economy in the world, ahead of even some European countries, like Norway and Belgium. Its size, its logistical ability to operate in multiple locations, and the abundance of poor workers around the world create ideal business conditions for maximizing shareholder profits and staying competitive in the global marketplace. For poorer countries like Bangladesh, securing a contract for a factory often means reducing or eliminating taxes, waiving labor and environmental regulations, and guaranteeing labor at a particular wage. These trends culminated with the establishment of export processing zones or free trade zones that have different rules from the rest of the country in order to lure corporations to establish factories there. According to political geographer Gabriel Popescu, "In 2007 there were an estimated 79,000 TNCs employing over one hundred million people worldwide, and 790,000 foreign affiliates."[49]

Despite the terrible working conditions and the concessions the government makes to foreign corporations, the factories provide jobs and income for people who would otherwise not have any. Advocates of free trade point to these benefits, and the employment of women particular (80 percent of employees in the Bangladesh garment sector are women), in order to argue that sacrifices are necessary for the country to make the transition into the industrialized world, a process that is termed *developmentalism*.[50] The developmentalism narrative argues that poor countries today should follow the same steps to development that Europe took in the past. Transitioning from an agricultural to an urbanized, industrial economy was the first step in Europe.[51] However, the difference is that when European countries made the transition, they were already the world's wealthiest nations; global corporations did not exist to take advantage of their position. Just as wages in early twentieth-century factories were minuscule, the pay in global factories today is often too low for workers to develop substantial wealth that would allow them to purchase goods made in the factories, let alone cars or new homes.

The era of globalization has allowed the wealth that once went to unionized workers in the United States and Europe to be shifted to corporations through outsourcing jobs. Furthermore, the conditions in factories are often horrendous, undoing a century of advances in workplace safety and environmental regulation. Finally, shipping goods across the ocean involves heavy usage of oil and gas, contributing to environmental damage. Nevertheless, workers, contained by borders and without other options, still take these jobs.

Not just a few bad apples

In 2015, the comedy news show *Last Week Tonight* did a report on the global fashion industry in which the host John Oliver, in his signature style, publicly shamed major apparel companies such as Children's Place, H&M, and Gap for their continued use of questionable production practices in factories around the world, with a particular focus on Bangladesh.[52] Oliver noted that these companies had been caught multiple times producing clothing in factories with child labor and horrendous working conditions. When confronted, the companies claimed they were unaware of the violations because their contract was with a primary factory, which then subcontracted the work to other factories. They promised to end the objectionable practices immediately. In fact, these repeated violations were predictable, part of the business model of these companies, and are the only way that clothing can be as cheap as it is. The segment ended with Oliver subcontracting the delivery of lunch to the companies' CEOs, with the promise that the food would be of the highest standard. However, he could not be held responsible for the actions of the subcontractors preparing and delivering the food. If they spit in the food or rubbed it against their private parts, it was beyond his control.

The show was alternatively devastating and funny, but Oliver—like many other critics of sweatshops abroad—was targeting the wrong actors. There is little doubt that these companies have made enormous profits by exploiting low-wage workers who, thanks to borders and immigration laws, have little choice but to stay and work in the only jobs available. Shaming these companies may damage their sales and force them to change their production methods, but other companies will rise in their place. In June 2015, Bangladesh charged Rana Plaza owner Sohel Rana and forty others with murder.[53] If convicted, they face the death penalty. Certainly, the worst global companies should be prosecuted, as should local factory owners. However, focusing on the "bad apples" of the global labor system risks distracting from the larger systemic problem. As the Human Rights Watch report puts it, "The poor and abusive working conditions in Bangladesh's garment factories are not simply the work of a few rogue factory owners willing to break the law. They are the product of continuing government failures to enforce labor rights, hold violators accountable, and ensure that affected workers have access to appropriate remedies."[54]

In this way, shaming individual companies is similar to shaming individual plantation owners during the slavery era:

forcing the most brutal plantation owners to practice slavery more humanely left in place the system of slavery. As long as labor is contained by borders and not protected by basic labor and environmental standards, the systems of exploitation will continue regardless of whether individual companies change their practices.

The problem is an issue of scale. In the 1930s, the US government had the ability to institute changes to the economy that would eventually lift the country out of the Depression. On this point, it does not matter whether you consider the effective measures to be more regulations, as the Keynesians do, or fewer, as free-marketers do. The US government had the ability to control the economy and impose changes that affected the economy as a whole. Today, the political tools are not in place to solve the problem. It is not necessarily a problem of political will; it is a systemic problem with how power is organized in the world. The problem is that borders artificially create different wages, labor pools, environmental regulations, taxes, and working conditions. Even if current American presidents wanted to enact sweeping regulations, they do not have the same ability Roosevelt had to confront the economic problem, because corporations and workers are no longer completely under US regulatory authority. While corporations are able to operate in many countries in order to take advantage of these differences, workers are usually contained by these borders and regulators are unable to enforce rules outside their jurisdiction. The problem crosses borders, but the solutions are contained by them.

From the free market Chicago School perspective, the crisis in the US economy in the post-1970s era was not the result of competition from foreign producers; the problem was that government interference in the economy had crippled US companies with burdensome regulations and high wages that made them uncompetitive. The solution, they argue, is to remove those regulations and labor protections in order to free up US corporations to produce goods and services more efficiently at lower costs. This would allow them to compete with foreign producers with lower production and labor costs. What the Chicago School overlooks is that the system of bordered states is itself an artificial limit on markets because it contains the movement of workers.

Keynesians question the social and moral costs of a race to the bottom on wages, labor conditions, and environmental conditions. If the problem is the discontinuity of regulations, why not raise standards everywhere? Free trade agreements probably make sense—if they are accompanied by the free movement of people. Restricting the movement of workers creates artificially low wages. If workers could move, wages would stabilize between the high wage in the United States and the low wage elsewhere. This would allow the economy to produce goods based on the real value of the work, without a low-wage subsidy artificially produced by borders. It is still not clear whether the Keynesian or Chicago School economic model works better at a global scale, because neither is in effect. Instead, the economy has been hampered by artificial barriers: the political borders that contain labor and regulators but not capital.

Chapter 7

Borders, Climate Change, and the Environment

The landscape of the southwestern United States, with vast deserts and scrublands occasionally crossed by craggy mountains, allows for sweeping and dramatic views of seemingly endless open space. The sense of a limitless place to roam created a home for thousands of Native Americans and later drew restless European migrants, who fought for political control of the land but never really controlled the vast landscape itself, where human impacts are less visible than in the rest of the United States. At first glance, the arid lands appear unable to support much wildlife, but a closer inspection finds many species thriving, from insects to large mammals. The larger animals that live in the desert Southwest include the javelina (a relative of the wild boar), mountain lions, bighorn sheep, coyotes, deer, tortoises, and jackrabbits. The animals that inhabit this land often have wide ranges, as they move through the sparse vegetation and dry landscape foraging for food. The lack of human impact on many of these lands makes the 6.4-meter (21-foot) US border fence, which is visible from many kilometers away, all the more jarring. The fence is designed to prevent the movement of only one species, humans, but it inevitably also disrupts the habitats of all the other large animals. The fence's construction includes small gaps at the bottom, 15 centimeters (6 inches) high, in order to allow insects and very small animals to pass through. However, anything larger than a small rodent is blocked by the fence in the same way that humans are.

In addition to animal habitats, the fence affects the runoff of water in the normally arid desert, which only gets rain in brief, heavy deluges. The water forms mighty rivers in arroyos as it rushes away. Organ Pipe Cactus National Monument, located in southwestern Arizona on the US–Mexico border, is a 1,338-square-kilometer (517-square-mile) UNESCO biosphere reserve that contains the only wild organ pipe cactus in the United States. All of the arroyos in the park run downhill, from north to south, into Mexico, but the fence on the border disrupts this process by blocking flows, snagging debris, and creating dams. A National Park Service report in the aftermath of a 2008 flood concluded that the design of the fence failed to accommodate the normal runoff patterns at the border and would affect the habitat of the organ pipe cactus by diverting floodwater away from Mexico and sending it horizontally along the border.[1] The report concludes that the fence would change vegetation in the area by allowing water to pool and altering sedimentation patterns. Over the longer term, the floodplain will change, as new arroyos develop that run parallel to the fence rather than into Mexico. Similar floods have occurred at other sites along the border fence, including in Nogales, Arizona, where flooding caused by the wall damaged cars and homes in 2008 and 2014.[2]

The full extent of the fence's damage to animals and the environment is unknown because of an unusual provision in the Real ID Act of 2005. The act created rules that standardized the data and security features on state-issued identity cards like driver's licenses, but it also had a provision that gave the Secretary of Homeland Security the ability to waive any federal laws necessary to build a wall on the border, even though the act itself had nothing to do with the border or building walls. When Congress passed the Secure Fence Act in 2006, which authorized the construction of the border fence, DHS secretary Michael Chertoff used the waiver authority from the previous act to waive thirty-seven laws in the construction of the fence. These included the Endangered Species

Act, the Clean Water Act, the Clean Air Act, the National Environmental Policy Act, the Migratory Bird Treaty Act, the Wilderness Act, the Wild and Scenic Rivers Act, and the Antiquities Act.[3] Many of these would have required environmental impact assessments and remediation for any damage to sensitive habitats, such as for the Sonoran desert tortoise, whose range in the Organ Pipe Cactus National Monument included a watering hole on the Mexican side of the border, or historical sites, such as Native American burial grounds.

There is little doubt that the hardening of borders often has a direct negative impact on the environment in border areas. The construction of walls and other defensive structures require clearing vegetation, leveling ground, and building roads and other infrastructure. During the construction of the wall in the West Bank from 2002 to 2007, Israel dug up tens of thousands of olive trees.[4] The Indian border fence blocked traditional elephant migration routes along the border with Bangladesh and funneled elephants to more populated areas. From 2002 to 2015, 226 people were killed by elephants and 62 elephants were killed by people, forcing the Indian government to reopen corridors for elephants to pass through the area.[5] Patrolling borders requires large deployments of agents, who trample through the landscape, disturbing vegetation. Because many borders are security zones, they tend not to be well maintained and often accumulate trash, debris, and the detritus left behind by previous migrants. Barbed wire and concertina wire are designed to snag clothing and human flesh, but they are also very good at capturing and entangling plastic bags. The wind and flowing water accumulate trash along the base of border infrastructure.

These examples of immediate environmental damage from hardening and militarizing borders are significant, but the ideology of borders and resources enclosures has broader effects on environmental degradation and climate change. Just as borders are used to limit the movement of the poor by creating pools of exploitable labor, they are used to control the environment by creating pools of exploitable resources, with rules on extraction and access that differ across territories. These enclosures allow some to use the earth's resources while restricting access and use by most others. The division of the earth into separate political jurisdictions means that the scale of decision-making (the state) does not match the scale of the system (the globe), which can produce overexploitation and exacerbate the challenge of addressing problems that cross borders. The impact of environmental change is uneven: wealthy industrialized states, which produce the majority of the greenhouse gases that drive climate change, have the resources available to ameliorate its worst effects. Furthermore, the guiding documents of the United Nations, ostensibly the best global venue to tackle the problem of environmental change, protect the absolute authority of states to make economic and environmental decisions within their borders, which precludes reaching a meaningful solution to the problem. The 2015 Paris Agreement on Climate Change, which is discussed in depth below, illustrates the damage absolute state sovereignty over environmental decisions does to the global environment and the limitations of the United Nations as a venue for global solutions.

Tragedy of the commons—or of enclosed extractivism?

In the late 1960s, Garrett Hardin, a professor of human ecology at the University of California at Santa Barbara, used the metaphor of the tragedy of the commons to describe the threat posed by growing populations and limited common resources.[6] He suggested that the tragedy is that individuals operating rationally in a system without regulation of common resources will put their individual needs above those of the group, leading to the depletion of the resource. This potential threat to common resources is often used to justify the enclosure of resources by bringing them into the sovereignty regime of the state and making them private property. In this view, state sovereign control over resources is preferable because the state has the ability to regulate the use of the resource and the incentive to protect the needs of the larger group over the individual. Similarly, private property protects resources because owners have an incentive to preserve their investment and prevent it from being completely destroyed.

In some instances, state sovereign authority over a resource can provide protection from exploitation by limiting access in order to prevent its overuse. This works when a particular resource or animal is predominantly within the territory of a state that has strong laws that are vigorously enforced. For example, in the United States, the Endangered Species Act of 1973 protects more than a thousand species by making it a crime to kill them or damage their habitats. The act works because the United States controls a vast territory, including large ranges of the habitats of the protected animals, and the enforcement mechanisms are strong enough to prevent most people from violating them.

Other scholars, including Elinor Ostrom, the Nobel Prize–winning political economist, are more critical of the "tragedy of the commons" thesis. Ostrom argues that the tragedy of the commons is based on false assumptions about human behavior that are not borne out by the evidence of how common resources have been historically protected.[7] She points to many historical examples of successful management of common resources and concludes that the success of a particular system depends on what the resource is, how plentiful it is, what norms are in place regulating individual behavior, and how strenuously regulations are communicated and enforced. Research demonstrates that private property, state control, and local management can each fail to prevent the destruction of common resources in different situations.[8] Coral reefs and fisheries are two examples of resources that have so far not been effectively protected through state conservation efforts. Marine protected areas create zones where fish species are protected and given time and space to reproduce. However, current marine protected areas are not large enough, close enough to each other, or numerous enough to protect most marine species. A study in 2006 found that 18 percent of coral reefs globally are in protected areas, but only 0.01 percent of those were in protected areas that completely restricted fishing and were well monitored to prevent poaching, large enough to cover a species' habitat, and close enough to other protected areas to cover the lifetime migration of the species.[9] The other 99.99 percent were at risk, without adequate protections.

The enclosure of the oceans as exclusive economic zones in the Law of the Sea (LOS) demonstrates how enclosures, which the "tragedy of the commons" thesis suggests will protect resources, can actually lead to more intensive exploitation. The problem with the LOS is that it is primarily focused on bringing untapped marine resources into the productive realm of the state, not on creating conservation areas. Article 61, clause 1 gives coastal states the exclusive right to "determine the allowable catch of the living resources in its exclusive economic zone." The LOS emphasizes that coastal states should use resources to their maximum or, in other words, "promote the objective of optimum utilization of the living resources in the exclusive economic zone." Article 61, clause 2 includes conservation as an obligation for the state, which should ensure that marine resources are measured and not overexploited, but it does not provide any funding to facilitate this or any penalties for not doing it. The coastal states are expected to determine what the maximum yields are and then patrol themselves to ensure they do not exceed them. It is akin to letting children determine how much candy they can eat each day and then trusting them to make sure they do not eat more than their allotted amount.

While some states like the United States and many European countries have worked to establish sustainable-catch quotas for their seas, others have not. Many states in Africa that do not have large-scale national fishing industries sell fishing rights in their exclusive economic zones to fleets from other states, mostly from Europe.[10] This creates a market to trade in the rights to fish these areas, which ensures that most fisheries are used to their full extent.[11] The result is that oceans are more heavily fished now than they were prior to the passage of the LOS. Whereas in 1980 only 15 percent of fisheries were overexploited, in 2010 32 percent were overexploited or depleted.[12] Some scholars have predicted that all fisheries will collapse in the next fifty years, in spite of, or perhaps because of, the enclosure of 44 percent of the oceans under the administration of states.

National parks, by contrast, are examples of successful state conservation efforts that protect wildlife from the threat of hunting and habitats from the destruction of development. William Cronon, professor of geography and history at the University of Wisconsin and author of *Nature's Metropolis*, and other scholars are nevertheless critical of these spaces, not because they are ineffective at protecting the wildlife and habitats within the park but due to the distinctions they create between inside and outside of conservation spaces.[13] National parks portray an idealized version of nature that does not leave space for humans in it. In the United States, prior to the creation of the parks, many of these areas were inhabited by Native Americans, who were part of the natural ecosystem. The Native American tribes—like the Blackfoot, who lived in the area that became Glacier National Park in Montana—lived off the land, hunting animals, foraging for berries and roots, and fishing in the streams. They functioned as predators, as a natural part of the ecosystem, in the same way that bears and wolves do today. When Glacier National Park was established, the Blackfoot were removed from their traditional lands and relocated to reservations outside the park boundaries. The removal of humans from the ecosystem is akin to removing other natural predators from the park. Today, if the Blackfoot go back to their traditional hunting grounds, they are treated as poachers. A similar process has played out in game reserves in Africa: for example, the removal of the nomadic San people from the Central Kalahari Game Reserve in Botswana beginning in the 1990s.[14] What seems like a noble idea—protecting wild areas—has detrimental consequences because it leaves no space for a natural and sustainable human presence in the ecosystem. Moreover, the creation of the parks as a protected natural space implies that all of the area outside the parks is unnatural and exploitable space. Protecting a pristine version of nature in bounded parks thus legitimates the extraction and destruction of all other spaces.

The tragedy of the commons is really the tragedy of resource destruction, which occurs when the enclosure of resources is combined with the ideology of extractivism. Naomi Klein, climate activist and bestselling author of *This Changes Everything*, defines extractivism as "the mentality that allowed so many of us, and our ancestors, to believe that we could relate to the earth with such violence in the first place—to dig and drill out the substances we desired while thinking little of the trash left behind, whether in the land and water where the extraction takes place, or in the atmosphere, once the extracted material is burned."[15] Economic and environmental ideologies have damaged the earth, Klein writes, by justifying clear-cutting forests, using open-pit mines, and pumping billions of gallons of toxic fluids into the earth to extract natural gas. The enclosure of common lands as private property is also an ineffective mechanism for protecting resources because it gives the owner the exclusive right to exploit the land for economic gain. State sovereignty and private property are prerequisites for capitalist extraction, with resource enclosures institutionalizing the ability of states and landowners to control land, use a resource exclusively, and develop, transform, and damage land, with little regard to the broader impacts of these activities.

The uneven geography of climate change

While climate change is global, its solutions are bounded by state borders and limited by the concept of private property. The Intergovernmental Panel on Climate Change (IPCC) assessment report, now in its fifth iteration, uses dispassionate but forceful language to summarize the current research on climate change. "Warming of the climate system is unequivocal," it states, "and since the 1950s, many of the observed changes are unprecedented over decades to millennia. The atmosphere and ocean have warmed, the amounts of snow and ice have diminished, sea level has risen, and the concentrations of greenhouse gases have increased."[16] The report lays out the overwhelming evidence of climate change, including rising air and sea temperatures, and rising sea levels. A range of factors affect atmospheric carbon dioxide levels—some anthropogenic, others natural—but regardless, these levels are the highest in the past 800,000 years and have increased 40 percent during the industrial era from fossil-fuel use and land-use changes.[17] Thirty percent of carbon dioxide is stored in the oceans, which changes the pH of the water through acidification, and there is already evidence of dissolving shells and damage to reefs. It is unclear how quickly marine species can adapt to more acidic water, but research on marine locations where natural vents release carbon dioxide into the oceans, creating zones of different levels of acidity, suggests that one-third of marine species will not survive in the acidic water predicted by the end of the century.[18]

From one perspective, borders have no impact on climate change, which is oblivious to the imagined territorial lines of state sovereignty and private property. Hurricanes destroy human settlements in the United States and the Philippines alike. Oceans take fish and marine debris all around the world. Rising sea levels will affect both countries that produce pollution and those that do not. Winds blow dust, pollution, and rains across borders. However, in other ways, borders have a key role to play in the phenomenon. There is a strong geographic pattern to where environmental pollution has historically been produced, where climate changes will have significant impacts on humans, and where geoengineering proposals to combat climate change will negatively affect the environment. Beginning with the Industrial Revolution, Europe and the United States have produced the majority of the carbon dioxide and other greenhouse gases that have been added to the environment by human activity. These places began large industrial and agricultural changes earlier and have utilized fossil fuels to a much larger extent than the people who live in the rest of the world. From 1800 to 1988, the so-called developed world, which represents about one-sixth of the world's population, produced 68 percent of all emissions.[19] Today, the carbon footprint of populations in developed societies is much higher than in other parts of the world, thanks to the history of industrialization, the consumption-based economy, and lifestyles that rely on cars, air conditioning, airplanes, and industrial agriculture—all of which have a large carbon footprint.

Data on per-capita emissions are available from the Energy Information Administration of the US Department of Energy.[20] The latest data, from 2011, show that residents of Qatar and the United Arab Emirates produce the most carbon dioxide, at over 44 metric tons per person per year. The United States produces 17.6 metric tons per person, and China's rapidly growing rate is 6.0 metric tons per person. The lowest three are Malawi, Mali, and Congo at 0.06, 0.05, and 0.04 metric tons per person respectively. In other words, a village of 1,100 people in Congo produces the same amount of carbon dioxide as one person in Qatar or three people in the United States. On a per-country basis (2009 figures), China is by far the largest producer, with 8.127 billion metric tons of carbon dioxide per year, followed by the United States at 5.483 billion. The entire continent of Africa, with a population of over 1.1 billion people, only produces 1.169 billion metric tons per year. Furthermore, just three countries—Algeria, South Africa, and Egypt—account for 68 percent of Africa's emissions, because they have economies based on oil or coal, which both produce substantial carbon dioxide emissions when burned.

Just as there is a geographical pattern to where emissions were produced historically and where they are produced today, climate models suggest that climate change will not affect the entire world equally.[21] Some areas may see cooling in the coming decades due to changing ocean currents, while others will be much hotter and dryer.[22] The IPCC report identifies sub-Saharan Africa and small island states as the most vulnerable to substantial negative environmental changes due to climate change—less rainfall for sub-Saharan Africa and sea-level rise for the island states—and they do not have the resources or infrastructure to adequately adapt to environmental changes.[23]

Perhaps the most immediate effects are felt by small island states.[24] The IPCC report identifies many risks for small island communities to their coastal, terrestrial, and human systems "from climate-related processes originating well beyond the borders of an individual nation or island."[25] The coastal risks are sea-level rise, shoreline erosion, acidification of surface waters, and degradation of fisheries, mangroves, and sea grasses. The risks to terrestrial systems include saline incursion degrading ecosystems, altitudinal species shift, incremental degradation of groundwater quality, and rapid salinization of groundwater. For human systems, the threats are general environmental degradation and loss of habitat in urban locations, reduced tourism, human susceptibility to climate-induced diseases, casualties and damage during extreme events, and relocation of communities/migration.[26] The report ranks these in terms of confidence of future events and ability to measure these changes. The highest confidence is in sea-level rise, coral bleaching, and species shift. Small islands will not necessarily be more affected than other coastal areas. Their extreme vulnerability is due to their level of dependence on coastal habitats for their homes and food and the lack of nearby alternative spaces to relocate to in the case of an extreme event. The term *climate refugee* is often used to describe people who will have to move in the future due to these climate changes, but the term *refugee*, as defined in the United Nations Convention on Refugees, is limited to someone who flees political, racial, or ethnic persecution, not environmental changes. The phrase *climate-induced migration* is more appropriate.[27]

The Maldives is one of the small island states that are perhaps the most at risk. It has a population of 350,000 people and consists of twenty-six coral atolls, ring-shaped islands around a lagoon, along a submarine ridge in the Indian Ocean, off the coast of India. The islands are stunningly beautiful, with sandy beaches and azure waters ringing small islands dotted with palm trees. The Maldives is very vulnerable, with an average height of only 1.5 meters (just under 5 feet) above sea level and a highest point of only 2.4 meters (almost 8 feet) above sea level. Sea level has risen by just under 3 millimeters (0.12 inches) per year since the 1990s; if it continues, this would mean that large sections of the Maldives will be underwater by the end of this century. Because of these threats, the government of the Maldives has pledged to be carbon neutral by 2020 and is a leader in small island states' effort to push for strict global limits on greenhouse-gas emissions.[28] However, the individual efforts of island states like the Maldives will not be enough. Because the climate is global, individual states alone cannot prevent environmental change; it must be done collectively.

Naomi Klein details an even more perverse possible consequence of climate change: the uneven impact of human efforts to use technologies to reverse global warming by artificially lowering the temperature of the earth. Some of the proposals are fantastical—for example, shooting cremated human remains into the atmosphere to block sunlight and free up cemetery space—but others, such as solar radiation management, have the backing of major philanthropists, including Bill Gates. Solar radiation management uses previous historical events that have resulted in the temporary cooling of the climate as a guide for strategies to reduce the earth's temperature to mitigate the impact of climate change. The most promising and feasible technology would mimic the effects of massive volcanic eruptions that emit sulfur and other particles into the atmosphere. Often dubbed the "Pinatubo Option," it is based on the global cooling that occurred in the year that followed the Pinatubo volcano's eruption in 1991, when temperatures dropped half a degree Celsius.[29] This suggested that it might be possible to lower the earth's temperature artificially by intentionally injecting these same compounds into the atmosphere. However, the eruption of Pinatubo and other major volcanoes did not simply have an impact on global temperatures: they also brought on dramatic reductions in rainfall in Africa and South Asia, which in turn produced drought, famine, and widespread death.

The Pinatubo Option represents a response to a global problem produced by wealthy countries that would most negatively affect poor countries that had little to do with climate change in the first place. Klein writes that this seems unbelievable, except that "we can imagine it because wealthy-country governments are already doing this, albeit more passively, by allowing temperatures to increase to levels that are a danger to hundreds of millions of people, mostly in the poorest parts of the world, rather than introducing policies that interfere with short-term profits."[30] The structural violence of borders concentrates the negative impacts of borders on more vulnerable places and contains the affected people to those areas through movement restrictions at borders.

There is still a relatively simple solution to the current climate crisis: reduce the rate of carbon dioxide and other greenhouse gases released by human activity dramatically by moving away from fossil fuels, reforming agricultural practices, and reducing the use of concrete. The problem is that much of the global economy is based on the availability of affordable and plentiful fossil fuels. Although the technologies exist to transform energy production and move away from oil and natural gas, doing so would be expensive and would negatively affect large corporations in the energy and transportation sectors.

The United Nations and the failure of global climate agreements

The United Nations appears to be the ideal venue to tackle the issue of climate change. Its purpose is to reach global agreements between states and it includes representatives of all of the states of the world. Indeed, all of the major climate meetings have occurred under the auspices of the UN, and it continues to hold yearly climate conferences in search of an elusive global agreement to reduce emissions and tackle the issue of environmental change. The most recent was the Paris Round in December 2015, which produced a global agreement on dealing with climate change that is significant, but lacks any enforcement mechanism and does not even mention the term *fossil fuels*. In order to understand why these meetings have failed, it is important to consider why the UN was established, what its purpose is, and whose interests it serves.

The UN is not a global government. It is a political institution designed to stabilize relations between states and prevent wars of territorial expansion. In the early twentieth century, as the system of sovereign states as bounded, territorial containers of power was becoming entrenched in Europe, there was no international body for arbitrating disputes between states. The first half of the twentieth century was a particularly unstable period, when the two world wars in Europe demonstrated the threat of expansionary wars.[31] After World War I, the League of Nations was established in order to provide some stability at the international level, but it was weak and quickly became irrelevant. In the United States, it was opposed by isolationists and nationalists, who were suspicious that it ceded American sovereignty to an outside authority, a concern that continues to undermine any efforts to make binding agreements at the global level. In the US Senate, the League was opposed by majority leader Henry Cabot Lodge and by Senator William Borah, whose impassioned speech invoking the Founding Fathers against joining the League in November 1919 brought some in the gallery to tears.[32] The Senate did not ratify the treaty and the United States never joined the League of Nations, which undermined the League's effectiveness as a global institution.

During World War II, it was clear that a much stronger international organization was necessary to maintain stability in the sovereign state system; the United Nations was established to serve this role. The first two articles of its charter explain that its goals of achieving global peace and stability will be achieved only through the mutual recognition of the boundaries of each member state. "Members should refrain in their international relations from the threat or use of force against the territorial integrity or political independence of any state," it declares. The implication here is that the organization as a whole should resist any movements that threaten the territorial integrity of another member state, meaning that the United Nations primarily reproduces the status quo in which the boundaries of currently existing sovereign states are recognized and protected by the other UN member states. The UN itself is expressly prohibited from meddling in the internal affairs of member states.

The organization's name includes the word *nations*, but the reality is that the UN is run by and through sovereign states. Although *nation* and *state* are often used interchangeably, they refer to different entities. A state is a political institution with a bureaucracy, territory, borders, and the sovereign right to create and enforce laws. A nation is a group of people who perceive that they have a shared connection to each other and to a land that entitles them to political control over that territory. There are many examples of groups such as the Kurds that consider themselves to be nations but do not control an independent state. The UN serves to institutionalize existing states as the legitimate sovereign authorities in bounded territories. The plight of so-called unrecognized states, places that have political control over a territory but lack external recognition of that control, shines a light on how this perpetuates the status quo. Examples of unrecognized states include Somaliland, the northern third of the failed state of Somalia, which has operated independently since 1991. Somaliland has held multiple elections with peaceful transfers of power and it has a currency, a military, and a police force, but it lacks the recognition of any other sovereign state or the United Nations.³³ States have to be recognized by other states to join the UN; by joining, a state agrees to recognize the boundaries and sovereignty of all the other member states. The UN's recognition of the territory and borders of Somalia when it joined in 1960 precludes the recognition of Somaliland as a separate state, even though Somaliland fulfills all the other typical characteristics of a state. Instead, the status quo of already existing states is maintained and protected above all other considerations.

Those in the United States who fear that the UN is a global government that will undermine US sovereignty misunderstand the UN's function. The UN was established by the leaders of the militarily and economically powerful states at the end of World War II and it functions to sustain their power. In fact, the UN is a very unequal institution that places most of the power in the hands of the five permanent members of the Security Council: China, France, Great Britain, Russia, and the United States. Far from threatening state sovereignty, its structure and purpose make any global agreement that requires the disaggregation of state control over environmental resources a nonstarter.

The 2015 Paris Agreement is the latest in a series of meetings and conferences organized by the United Nations to address the issue of climate change. The first major global environmental summit was the 1972 Conference on the Human Environment, held in Stockholm, Sweden, which led to the creation of the UN Environmental Program. Twenty years later, the first United Nations Conference on Environment and Development, commonly referred to as the Rio or Earth Summit, was held in Rio de Janeiro, Brazil. Since 1995, the UN has held annual meetings on climate change, with the meeting in Paris representing the twenty-first iteration. At each of these meetings there is broad agreement that the climate is changing, that often the poorest and most vulnerable will be the most affected, that something must be done, and on what steps could be taken to reverse some of the most damaging human impacts. However, relatively little happens due to the political challenges created by bounded territories of absolute sovereignty.

The original documents produced at the Rio Earth Summit in 1992 continue to frame the debate about humans' impact on the environment. The three key documents were Agenda 21, which established non-binding goals for reducing poverty and conserving resources, the Rio Declaration, and the United Nations Framework Convention on Climate Change. The Rio Declaration epitomizes the problem with addressing climate change through the UN and the sovereign state system.[34] It includes twenty-seven principles meant to guide future climate-change negotiations. The preamble highlights the importance of "protecting the integrity of the global environmental and developmental system, recognizing the integral and inter-dependent nature of the Earth, our home."[35] However, the second principle reiterates the centrality of state sovereignty over environmental decisions. States have "the sovereign right to exploit their own resources pursuant to their own envi-ronmental and developmental policies," it reads, "and the responsibility to ensure that activities within their jurisdiction or control do not cause damage to the environment of other States."[36] This principle ensures that any global environmental agreements will not infringe on an individual state's need to damage the environment in extracting resources. While the second clause of the principle does identify a responsibility for damage beyond the state's borders, it reiterates that within its borders each state has the absolute authority to use its ter-ritory as it chooses. All of the remaining principles operate within the confines of bordered states and are not meant to create a global set of regulations. Consequently, as global agreements have been forged over the past twenty-five years, individual states have opted out of them, failed to implement them, or promised only minimal changes, which undermines the entire premise.

The United Nations Framework Convention on Climate Change was also produced at the 1992 Rio conference. The original convention includes neither benchmarks for individ-ual states nor enforcement mechanisms. Instead, it established a framework for negotiating future protocols to reduce green-house gases by creating a system for monitoring greenhouse gases on a state-by-state basis. In 1997, delegates agreed to the Kyoto Protocol, which established benchmarks for developed countries (so-called Annex I countries) to reduce green-house gases. The agreement excluded international aviation and shipping—both major omissions—but requires Annex I countries to reduce emissions to 8 percent below 1990 bench-mark levels. The EU as a whole has met these targets, with its emissions now an average of 20 percent below 1990 levels.[37] The United States signed the treaty but never ratified it. In 1997, the US Senate voted 95 to 0 for a bill that stated that the Senate was "against any international agreement that: 1) did not require developing countries to make emission reduc-tions and 2) would seriously harm the economy of the United States."[38] Nevertheless, the United States has also seen a decline in emissions over the past decade and is near its 1990 baseline.[39] The Kyoto Protocol was extended in 2012 in Doha, Qatar, with new targets for a 20 percent reduction from 1990 levels through 2020, although the majority of the previous signatories—including most European countries, Russia, and Brazil—did not join the new agreement. Only 59 countries ratified it out of the 144 required to bring it into force.[40]

Before the Paris talks, each of the global climate summits of the past twenty-five years followed a similar narrative arc, which usually begins a few months before the summit with hopeful reports that there is broad agreement on the issues at hand and the immediate need to address climate change.[41] In many cases, the major players announce a new initiative prior to the meetings, which seems to indicate willingness to act and a commitment to the issues. In the days before the meeting, reports are optimistic and use phrases like *frameworks*, *broad outlines*, and *general agreement*, but always include the caveat that the final details must be settled at the event. After the first day of the meeting, the hopeful tone starts to fade away and the stories emphasize the challenges that remain to be overcome. Inevitably, one of the powers reformulates its posi-tion, which changes the entire discussion at the meeting. On the penultimate day, there are reports of meetings stretching late into the night as delegates look for points of agreement to salvage something from the event. On the final day, all of the participants sign onto a watered-down accord that essentially indicates that all of the parties agree that a deal could not be reached, but it is critically important to continue to work together on the issue. The London *Telegraph* described the 2014 talks in Lima this way: "Inevitably, like just about every negotiating session before it, the Lima talks teetered on the brink of breakdown before—after three days and two nights of non-stop bargaining—they concluded by agreeing just about the bare minimum needed to keep going for another year."[42] In the days after the conferences, there are a series of articles about "why the UN Climate Conference failed."[43]

The 2015 talks in Paris followed this pattern, with early optimism giving way to concessions and an extension of the talks into an extra day. They eventually diverged from this narrative in that they were generally hailed as a success, at least by the governments involved and the media. President Obama said, "We succeeded. We came together around the strong agreement the world needed. We met the moment."[44] The agreement does go beyond the previous twenty attempts at a global accord on climate change because it involves pledges from all of the states in the world and codifies the goal of keeping global temperatures within two degrees Celsius of the preindustrial average yearly temperature. At the core of the agreement are the Intended Nationally Determined Contributions (INDC) that each country is expected to produce and promises for the amount of reductions each country will make. "This agreement," Obama said, "represents the best chance we have to save the one planet that we've got."

James Hansen, a former NASA scientist and climate activist, was dismissive of the deal, calling it "a fraud."[45] It is a fraud because, although it has all the trappings of a global agreement on climate change with pledges, language about the importance of keeping global temperatures lower, and a fund to help disadvantaged states, there is very little substance in the resulting document. The first slippery part is the INDC, which will be determined by each state on its own, not by a global formula or based on an objective analysis of how large the reductions need to be to reach the modest goal of two degrees Celsius. The agreement does not suggest appropriate reduction levels. The goal is the second problematic part of the agreement, because many scientists and small island states were pushing for a ceiling of 1.5 degrees Celsius. The third problem is that goals from each state do not have to be ambitious—and they do not have to be met. Analyses of the INDCs already announced by over 150 countries indicate that they are not even significant enough to reach the modest two-degree goal. The fourth problem is that there are neither independent measurements of each country's progress towards its goals nor enforcement mechanisms if states do not reach them. States are asked to self-report, which can easily be manipulated. This weakness was confirmed in November 2015 when China acknowledged that it had been underreporting admissions by 17 percent, or the equivalent of a billion additional metric tons of carbon dioxide per year.[46] Finally, airplanes and shipping are exempted from the rules and the terms *fossil fuels*, *oil*, and *natural gas* are not mentioned a single time in the document.

The Paris Agreement demonstrates the role of the UN precisely and illustrates why leaders of UN member states hail the agreement as a resounding success. The UN is a venue for states to meet and act to pursue their individual interests. In this instance, they came together to make an agreement that symbolizes their joint commitment to do something about climate change. However, the details of the agreement conform to all of the previous agreements that continue to give individual states all of the authority to make decisions on the environment in their territory. Thus the agreement is about voluntary goals that are neither monitored by an outside body nor enforced by any sanctions if they are not met. The agreement allows states to continue to monopolize the authority to make environmental, political, and economic decisions within their territory while simultaneously appearing to acquiesce to global goals to protect the climate. It's the kid with the candy jar once again.

Borders, scale, and privilege

The problem is neither our knowledge of climate change nor the recognition by most leaders in the world that something needs to be done. The problem is that the bordered containers of power in the world—states—and the venue for making agreements—the United Nations—give too much weight to the individual sovereignty of states and do not adequately represent the planet-wide needs of the earth.[47] The tragedy of enclosed extractivism is that what is best for a small group of people in a small piece of land does not match what is best for the whole of humanity.[48] Joe Nevins, a professor of geography at Vassar College, uses the term *ecological privilege* to describe advantages that are built on past exploitation and that allow some people to continue to use the environment in a more intensive way. Ecological privilege "leads to, for those who enjoy it, greater options, access to and control over resources, social power, and socioeconomic and biophysical security," he writes.[49] The term describes the right for someone to continue to use the environment simply because they have always done so, and also describes the system of state sovereignty and capitalist extraction that allows and encourages them to do so.

As long as the economic interests of individual states do not coincide with the larger environmental needs of the world, a meaningful agreement on climate change will not be reached. After all, the UN, which is the primary institution for climate negotiations, preserves the sovereign rights of states over the needs of the global environment. As long as the text of climate-change agreements prioritizes this idea, a way of combating this global phenomenon will not be reached until it is too late.

Conclusion

Movement as a Political Act

Are humans defined primarily by our attachments to place or by movement? One way of thinking about humanity is to see humans as a sedentary species with deep ancestral connections to homelands and nations.[1] Places play a significant role in how we situate ourselves in our families, in our communities, and in the world.[2] We are educated by our country's schools, learn our national language, culture, and traditions, and are protected (or harmed) by our country's police, courts, and military. We wear our national colors with pride when we sing our country's anthem at the Olympics.[3] The global political system is based on the idea that each nation should have political control over their homeland in order to determine what rights are guaranteed, how the land and resources can be used, and who can visit the nation-state.[4] In this view, borders are a natural part of the world because states have the right to protect their people, land, and resources from threats on the outside.

However, movement is also a critical part of humanity and the modern condition. At some distant point in the past, all humans were hunter-gatherers who moved with animal migrations and seasonal sources of food. Nomadic peoples, from the Mongols of Central Asia to the Bedouins of the Middle East, were central players in the history of the world, although their version of events was never recorded.[5] Travelers like Ibn Battuta and Marco Polo explored distant places. The wealth and power of early European states were built on long-distance trade and movement, and globalization today is premised on goods and services moving around the world, connecting producers and consumers in distant places. We have bicycles, cars, subways, high-speed trains, and airplanes to take us long distances. Movement is a central part of our daily lives.

The conflict between these two different versions of humanity lies at the core of this book. Tim Cresswell, geographer and author of *On the Move,* identifies it as the defining characteristic of the present day: "Mobility is central to what it is to be modern. A modern citizen is, among other things, a mobile citizen," he writes. Mobility symbolizes the freedoms of modernity, from the tourism industry to car culture, that define the character of contemporary America. "At the same time it is equally clear that mobility has been the object of fear and suspicion, a human practice that threatens to undermine many of the achievements of modern rationality and ordering," Cresswell adds.[6] At borders, mobility is violently restricted through laws that prioritize citizens' rights over human rights, walls that funnel migrants to dangerous crossing points, and a border security infrastructure that results in thousands of deaths every year. The direct and structural violence of borders forecloses the opportunity for many people to move.

The system of states, borders, and resource enclosures is embedded in our culture and our way of life and permeates many aspects of our existence, to the point that it is difficult to imagine life outside of it. But the past two hundred years have included major social changes that were previously unthinkable as people have collectively resisted injustices in the world, including slavery, colonialism, lack of universal suffrage, and South Africa's apartheid system. Today we take it for granted that these practices were unjust and it was only a matter of time before they collapsed, although at one point change seemed impossible. The current system of borders is no different.

The state as a boundary-making institution

The conflict between mobility and order is not unique to the modern world. It is a persistent theme from early human history through the present. From the moment that some humans began to settle down, grow crops, and collect resources in fixed locations, the movement of other humans was seen as a threat. The interaction between sedentary people and mobile people is critical to understanding the function of the state. The state is a boundary-making institution that legitimizes the exclusion of others from land, resources, wealth, and opportunity through legal regimes and military power. States make exclusive claims to land and resources, define who has access by creating and monitoring social boundaries of belonging, and enforce these exclusions with legally sanctioned violence, such as the right of the police to use force. The structural violence of borders is at the foundation of the state in its role as a collector, protector, and exploiter of resources and labor.

Previous theories of the state have identified the mechanisms of state power and authority, but have not emphasized the role of movement restrictions. UCLA sociologist Michael Mann draws on the work of sociologist and political theorist Max Weber to argue that a state is a centralized bureaucracy in a territory in which sovereignty is defined by a monopoly on the legitimate use of violence.[7] Italian philosopher Giorgio Agamben draws on political theorist Carl Schmitt to argue that the true power of sovereignty lies in the exception—in the ability to maintain a system of laws that apply to everyone but the sovereign, who can kill potential threats to the state without consequences.[8] Marxist theorists of political economy, such as geographer David Harvey, see the state as an institution that mediates the accumulation of wealth and perpetuates the hegemony of a capitalist elite.[9]

These theories capture part of the practice of the state, but miss the critical role played by boundaries. Walls, borders, maps, properties, identity documents, and enclosure laws are technologies of governance that are fundamentally about controlling and excluding. In the past, rulers and states used slavery and other coercive practices to control the movement of people within the state to ensure a stable supply of labor and troops for battle. It was only under the unique parameters of the age of colonization that the poor of Europe were briefly encouraged to move in relatively large numbers to new places. Throughout the twentieth century, states reasserted their ability to regulate the movement of the poor as more sophisticated passports and visa systems were put in place and more countries began to patrol their borders for unauthorized migration. The hardening and militarization of borders does not signal the retreat of sovereign authority; it signals the expansion of the ability of states to monitor and regulate movements in their territories and beyond. The rearticulation and expansion of sovereign authority means that it is no longer necessary to maintain the internal-external distinction between the police and the military as they maintain the boundaries of the state and of private property.

However, rulers and states are not seeking to prevent movement completely. Quite the opposite: they rely on the movement of goods and services to produce the wealth that sustains their power. Their opening up is evident in the proliferation of bilateral and multilateral free trade agreements, the global trade rules established at the World Trade Organization, and the creation of free trade zones in countries around the world. These changes allow corporations to establish factories in the cheapest places possible with minimal tax obligations and reduced environmental and labor regulations, which are critical to the functioning of the capitalist economic system and the maintenance of wealth.[10] The wealthy, as well, are able to move freely across the globe in order to manage these long-distance trading networks and to spend their money on consumer goods and services through tourism. The conflict over movement is really between what rulers and states categorize as "good" and "bad" movements, between movements that are benign, regulated, observed, allowed, and taxed and movements that are threatening, illicit, unseen, unapproved, and untaxed. The fundamental conflict of modernity is allowing "good" movements while preventing "bad" movements.[11]

Residents of wealthy countries perceive that they are freer to move around than in the past, but the reality for the majority of the people in the world mirrors previous eras' restrictions on movement. The overt coercion of state-sanctioned slavery is largely in the past, but the poor are still contained in developing countries and forced, by lack of other options, to work for very low wages to make products to benefit the wealthy.[12] Just as a serf or a slave could not move to another plantation to offer his or her work, laborers today are contained by borders and therefore wages are artificially suppressed. From the earliest states through the nineteenth century, labor was captured *within states* through slavery and serfdom. After a brief era of relatively free movement for the poor, today labor is captured *between states* through the global border regime of identity documents, border patrols, walls, and violence.

Displacing the nation

The place-based version of history is not natural and eternal; it is a technology of governance akin to a wall, a property deed, and a border guard that legitimates the concentration of wealth in the hands of a few and protects the privileges that have accrued through the enclosure of land and resources. Borders and lines on maps are not a representation of preexisting differences between peoples and places; they create those differences. Andrew Abbott, a sociologist at the University of Chicago, suggests that "we should not look for boundaries of things, but things of boundaries," which is to say that boundaries do not mark the edges of already existing things; the thing comes into being by placing boundaries.[13] The ideas of private property and bounded state territories emerged with the creation of modern maps. Maps of the modern sovereign state system institutionalize the notion that people fit neatly into categories, these categories fit neatly into homelands, and these homelands unambiguously should determine each individual's fate on the earth.

Although the deployment of new technologies and the use of military strategies and tactics at borders have increased the number of deaths through violence by border agents and by funneling migrants to more dangerous routes, the technologies themselves are not the primary cause of the violence. They only expand the ability of states and their agents to enforce the boundaries of territory and identity. The underlying logics of racism, nationalism, and groupism create conditions in which it is acceptable to treat other human beings in a dehumanizing and violent manner. Rogers Brubaker, a professor of sociology at UCLA, defines *groupism* as "the tendency to take discrete, sharply differentiated, internally homogeneous and externally bounded groups as basic constituents of social life, chief protagonists of social conflicts, and fundamental units of social analysis."[14] The preference for the in-group draws on a sense of family and community by creating a place where an individual belongs. It also emphasizes the threat posed by others who are not members of the group.

The distinction between inside and outside, between native and foreigner, pervades the political discourse in countries around the world because it is part of the foundation of the state as an institution. The place-based version of humanity plays a powerful role in the contemporary public discourse in many countries, as migrants are represented as a threat to the economic, cultural, and political system of the state. The EU migration crisis that began in 2015 has resulted in xenophobic and exclusionary responses that emphasized the right of the state to protect the cultural integrity of its population. In the United Kingdom, in addition to strict immigration quotas and controls already in place, Prime Minister David Cameron pledged to keep net immigration under 100,000 people per year by limiting visas, increasing taxes on businesses that employ migrants, and raising minimum-wage thresholds. After the 2015 election, Cameron created an Immigration Taskforce to reduce the number of migrants.[15] In France, the National Front party has an anti-immigration platform and is increasingly successful in the polls. The party's leader, Marine Le Pen, has compared migrants to barbarian invasions, saying, "Without any action, this migratory influx will be like the barbarian invasion of the fourth century, and the consequences will be the same."[16] In June 2015, French border police blocked the transport of several hundred migrants at the Italian border, angering Italian officials, who have dealt with a large share of migrant arrivals.[17] In Denmark, the anti-migrant Danish People's Party surged to unexpected second place in the June 2015 elections by calling for reinstituting border checkpoints, reducing aid for asylum seekers, and protecting spending on social programs for Danish citizens.[18] Some towns in Denmark passed rules requiring that pork be served in school lunches, as a direct rebuke to efforts to make meals acceptable to Muslim diets. "The Danish People's Party is working nationally and locally for Danish culture, including Danish food culture," explained Party spokesperson Martin Henriksen. "And that means we are also fighting against Islamic rules and misguided considerations dictating what Danish children should eat."[19]

It doesn't end there. In the United States, presidential candidate Donald Trump framed his campaign around protecting Americans from the threat of migration, calling for a wall on the entire Mexican border and a complete ban on Muslim immigration. The xenophobic response to migrants is not only present in wealthy "Western" countries, and it is not just directed toward particular ethnic or racial groups. Saudi Arabia expelled 160,000 Ethiopian migrants between November 2013 and February 2014.[20] The initial response by Malaysia, Indonesia, and Thailand to Rohingya refugee boats was to refuse to provide aid and to push the boats back to sea. In April 2015, six migrants were killed in riots and violence in South Africa that targeted people from Zimbabwe.[21] In June 2015, the Dominican Republic began to deport hundreds of thousands of migrants from Haiti, including children of migrants who did not speak Creole and had never been to Haiti.[22]

These responses to migration draw on fantasies of national purity and a fear of change that is exploited by politicians. The exclusion of others from resources and opportunity is based on the idea that the in-group should be protected no matter what, with little regard for what effect it might have on the other and without questioning why there is a distinction between "us" and "them" in the first place. Rather than hard lines around nations of people and their homelands, political borders are systems for controlling land and resources and limiting the movement of people. The "nations" they enclose are not long-term historical realities, but new political communities that developed with the emergence of states and borders. In Foucault's terms, maps of bordered territorial states are regimes of truth that establish what is true and legitimate in society. They justify some claims to land and history, while marking others as false and not worthy of consideration. These regimes are not fundamental truths that are universal; they are a set of agreements within a particular society that establish a set of rules to decide what is true, but it does not have to be that way.

Challenging borders and citizenship

The answer to violent borders could be a world without states, hierarchies, and capitalism. However, incremental changes can often be more effective, and are more achievable than holding out hope for a completely different world.[23] "The struggle to end apartheid in South Africa did not result in that country's disappearance," writes geographer Joe Nevins. "There is a need for a radical redefinition of what the nation-state is because, in its present form, control of movement across its territorial boundaries is one of its fundamental attributes. What this redefinition might look like is an open question, but at the very least it should embrace the ideal of all people, regardless of national origins, having a right to work and reside within the boundaries of any nation-state."[24]

As with many critical projects, this book has focused on identifying the problems with movement restrictions and resources enclosures. This penultimate section outlines three principles that are a basis for moving towards a world of equality of movement and access to resources and opportunities.

Free movement between states

The most immediate step that could be taken to address wealth inequality globally is opening borders to allow free movement.[25] This would release the poor from the trap of slums and moderate the vast inequalities in wages between wealthy and poor regions of the earth. It would also dramatically reduce the numbers of unnecessary deaths at borders. There is a long history of expanding the rights of citizenship to include people who were previously excluded from membership in the state.[26] The earliest states, such as the French and English monarchies of the Middle Ages, essentially protected the rights of one family. Over time these rights were extended to the wealthy aristocracy, to landowners, and eventually to all men. As liberal democratic states like the United States and many European countries have provided equal treatment to all individuals in the public sphere, their membership has been expanded to include many people that were once not considered citizens. It would have seemed inconceivable in the 1790s that women and slaves would be allowed to vote in the United States. It is reasonable to suggest that this be expanded to include human beings generally. One day, denying equal protection based on birthplace may well seem just as anachronistic and wrong as denying civil rights based on skin color, gender, or sexual orientation.

Indeed, the founding political documents of many states suggest this change would signify a more literal reading of some of the clauses. Although states have traditionally defended the rights of their citizens, the foundational documents are more aspirational. For example, the second paragraph of the United States' Declaration of Independence begins, "We hold these truths to be self-evident, that all men are created equal, that they are endowed by their Creator with certain unalienable Rights, that among these are Life, Liberty and the Pursuit of Happiness." If all of humanity is created equally and has an unalienable right to liberty, then that should include the liberty to move. The 1791 French Constitution specifies that the natural right to liberty includes freedom of movement. Under "Title I: Fundamental Provisions Guaranteed by the Constitution," after three primary provisions focused on equal protection under the law, the document states: "The constitution guarantees likewise as natural and civil rights: Liberty to every man to come and go without being subject to arrest or detention, except according to the forms determined by the constitution." The wording is clear: "every man" has the right "to come and go." Removing restrictions on movement at borders is compatible with the founding documents of France, the United States, and many other countries.

The shaky logical foundation of the current system of restrictions at borders is apparent in how the Universal Declaration of Human Rights addresses the issue of movement. The declaration was adopted by the United Nations General Assembly in 1948 as a statement of the rights to which all humans are entitled. Although nonbinding, it serves to define the fundamental rights guaranteed in the UN Charter and consequently plays a significant role in international law. The document has thirty articles and includes guarantees that everyone is born free and has the right to life, liberty, and security. It also bans slavery, cruel and unusual punishments, and torture. Article 13 addresses movement: "(1) Everyone has the right to freedom of movement and residence within the borders of each state; (2) Everyone has the right to leave any country, including his own, and to return to his country."[27] The right to movement within a sovereign state across local administrative borders is protected, as is the right to leave any country and enter your home country. However, movement into all other sovereign states is restricted. The two ideas are logically incompatible.[28] If freedom of movement is a human right, it should apply around the world, not just within individual states. Conversely, if states have the right to limit movement, they should be able to do so within their state territory as well as between them.

Consider this example. The US state of Maryland has the highest median household income at approximately $70,000 per year, double the rate of the neighboring state of West Virginia. Furthermore, West Virginia is often stereotyped as having a "country" culture that does not match the progressive Northeast. Maryland and West Virginia share a border, so imagine if the governor of Maryland decided to build a wall, set up internal checkpoints, and begin to deport the poorer and culturally different people of West Virginia. This sounds ludicrous—mostly because, within countries, the right to move trumps the rights of local political communities to limit access.[29] No matter how much Maryland might want to protect its economic wealth, jobs, and culture from the poor, unemployed, and culturally different residents of West Virginia, it cannot. Nevertheless, it seems normal that countries can do the exact same thing for the same reasons—to protect jobs, wealth, and culture. That sense of normalcy needs to be disrupted.

Perhaps the largest impediment to opening borders and allowing free movement is the fear that opening borders evokes in many people about the potential for economic, social, and security disruptions from a flood of migrants that would overwhelm wealthy countries. The fear of others is a powerful discourse that motivates people to act violently towards others who are perceived as a threat to their way of life. Opening borders for free movement would cause disruptions as the wealth, opportunity, and privileges that have accrued through the state system were partially undone. There were similar concerns about Eastern Europeans flooding Western Europe in 2004 when Hungary, Poland, and seven other countries were admitted to the European Union, but they turned out to be unfounded.[30] As the US example above demonstrates, there is already a sharp wealth gap between Maryland and West Virginia that has not resulted in massive population movement. Part of the reason is that many people prefer to remain in a place that is culturally comfortable. Another part is that many migration decisions are based on economic factors: if too many people tried to move, there would not be any jobs, which would dissuade future migrants. Finally, potential inconveniences to residents of wealthy states are not a justifiable reason to continue to enforce movement restrictions on the poor. Indeed, white South Africans, white Southerners, and virtually everyone who has found themselves in a privileged position based on the exploitation of others have made similar arguments in order to perpetuate their particular systems of inequality.

There are already a number of scholars and public officials recommending these types of changes to immigration controls.[31] In a few weeks over the spring of 2015, David Laitin, a professor of political science at Stanford, and Marc Jahr, the former director of the New York City Housing Development

Corporation, proposed allowing Syrian refugees to resettle Detroit, a city whose infrastructure and housing was designed for a much larger population than it currently has, while Phillip Legrain, a former advisor to the president of the European Commission, made the economic case for opening Europe's borders.[32] In Europe, the need to add more workers to the labor force is particularly pressing as aging populations and low birth rates strain social welfare programs. These commentators draw on growing evidence that migration has no impact on the employment rates of receiving states because, although new migrants do take jobs, they also create more jobs by contributing to the economy through spending. They pay taxes to the government, they buy food and clothes, and they pay for transportation. All of these activities produce more jobs for everyone. Studies of migration confirm this finding: Eastern Europeans moving to Western Europe after EU expansion, Mexican migrants moving to the United States, Jews from around the world moving to Israel.[33] More workers mean more jobs.

Global rules for working conditions

Many of the gains made by workers in the United States and Europe in the middle of the twentieth century are currently undermined by the lack of protections for workers in other parts of the world. The Chicago School of economic thought is right that the most efficient way for business to operate is in a free market with minimal government intervention, but there are historical examples of what that world looks like. It looks like *The Jungle*; it looks like the poverty, despair, and death at factories like the Rana Plaza in Bangladesh. Certainly this approach provides freedom and opportunity for some to pursue individual success—with all the caveats about access, upbringing, education, and networks—but at what cost? Instead of a race to the bottom as many corporations and

Chicago School thinkers suggest, in which worker protections are repealed to make companies in the US and EU more competitive, worker protections should be expanded to other countries around the world.

In addition to the freedom to move across borders, this means a global minimum wage, global standards for working conditions, global social safety nets for the poor, and global environmental standards. These basic regulations would prevent corporations from playing different countries against each other to get the lowest wages possible and would encourage corporations to locate factories where they make economic sense. Over time, such a change would create a global consumer base to buy products. It would slow the flow of jobs out of wealthy countries, because at some point moving jobs will no longer be as economically advantageous. It would improve living standards globally, as people would have enough money to support their families and send their children to school. In the short term it would hurt corporate profits, but in the long term it would create consumers globally, which would provide vast new markets for goods. A global minimum wage would go a long way to stabilizing wages in both wealthy and poor countries.

The idea has been proposed by many, including Nobel Peace Prize recipient Muhammad Yunus in the aftermath of the Rana Plaza disaster.[34] A global minimum wage would have to be adjusted to different countries around the world according to local prices, with perhaps 50 percent of the median wage in each country as a starting point. The good news is that, just as migration does not affect employment levels, studies have found that minimum wages have no discernible effect on employment.[35] The global rules for labor should also include provisions about working conditions, including limits on total hours and basic standards for conditions in factories, such as safe work conditions and protections for workers who report violations. These protections could include health care, workers' compensation for injuries sustained on the job, and other social services. Limiting working hours would also provide more jobs. If a typical worker in Bangladesh or China goes from sixty hours per week to forty, that would require an increase in employees to make up the additional hours.[36] Creating a basic set of rules for global working conditions would provide benefits to workers in the United States and European Union by making outsourcing much less attractive, and in poorer countries like Bangladesh and Ghana by providing jobs that pay enough to lift workers out of poverty. Furthermore, improved wages and conditions in poor countries would reduce workers' desire to move, which would help to soften the potential migrations that would come with free movement. As Friedrich Hayek suggests in *The Road to Serfdom*, as long as labor and environmental regulations affect all businesses equally, they are compatible with capitalism.

Global rules for environmental protection and limits on private property

The environmental violence of borders requires global regulations that limit activities that produce damage and incorporate their true costs. In order to make this possible, we must rethink the idea that states have the exclusive right to make environmental decisions in their territories. The environment does not respect borders and neither should human efforts to use and protect the earth. The structure and purpose of the United Nations make it difficult to achieve this goal through the existing international institutional infrastructure. However, it is also difficult to imagine how a global agreement—which requires at least two parties—can be achieved without the participation of states and the UN. Perhaps a new institutional infrastructure dedicated to the environment needs to be created that has the ability to overrule state sovereignty on issues that affect the global environment.

In addition to strict limits on harmful resource extraction and pollution, some of the funds raised through taxes and fines on these practices should be used to rehabilitate environments damaged by human activity, particularly those that defy the normal state-based model of responsibility. For example, the plastic pollution floating in the Pacific Ocean, often dubbed the Great Pacific Garbage Patch, is the result of the activities of humans in all of the areas surrounding the Pacific Ocean, as well as a massive tsunami. However, the debris gathers in the Pacific gyre, which is outside the jurisdiction of every sovereign state. Due to its remote location, it is caused by everyone but the responsibility of no one. Future global environmental agreements must address these supra-state issues by aligning political decision-making regarding the environment with the scale of environmental issues.

The economic and environmental violence of resource enclosures extends to the idea of private property. Just as the idea of states and nations often appears natural and eternal, it is difficult to think outside the bounded space of property. However, the rights of property owners to limit movement over the earth, exclusively control resources, and exploit their property have similar consequences as the idea of state sovereign control over territory. Consequently, a truly progressive reorientation of global politics would also include changes to the notion of private property. There certainly needs to be a rethinking of the right of property owners to exploit the resources on their property without limits. It could mean that property rights are not indefinite but return to the commons after a period of time or the death of the property owner. By changing the way land use is regulated, the use and abuse of the earth can be reformed.

These principles could not be put in place overnight. The global infrastructure of border security is vast and is supported by the strong economic interests of military and government contractors in the border security sector. These corporations have a vested interest in maintaining the status quo of militarized, hardened borders that continue to fill their coffers. Other powerful corporations extract resources based on the idea of private property and use differential labor and environmental regulations across borders to create the most favorable business conditions possible. However, a similar type of inertia surrounded past economic and political inequality. The systems were entrenched and supported by an economic system that perpetuated their existence, but eventually they were undone. Their collapse began through the acts of individuals who challenged the established order and brought the underlying inequality into view.

Movement as a political act

Although they are separated by four hundred years of history, Captain Pouch and his Diggers and Levellers, who rebelled against the enclosure of common lands in the Midlands Revolt, and migrants like Isaac and Gifty, the Ghanaian family who fled poverty in search of a better life in Europe, share a similar problem and made similar choices to resolve it. Both found themselves contained by lines on a map that restricted their ability to move and that protected the wealth and privilege of others. Both also refused to abide by the artificial boundary—in the same way that Harriet Tubman refused to abide by the system of slavery and fugitive slave laws, Mahatma Gandhi refused to abide by the laws of British colonialism, and Nelson Mandela refused to abide by the South African system of apartheid. The Diggers and Levellers contested exclusionary lines on the map by digging up the hedges and removing the evidence of the boundary on the ground. The migrants of today dig under, go around, climb over, or cut their way through the fences, walls, and security infrastructure that mark the edges of the global border regime.

In response to their refusal to accept their own unjust exclusion, they are met with the full violence of the state. In the Midlands Revolt, this refusal cost the lives of more than forty rebels. Their leaders were put to death and then quartered as a warning for others to abide by the new system of enclosures. At the edges of the global border regime, more than 40,000 people have lost their lives in the past ten years. The leaders of countries around the world hope that the construction of new fences, the hardening of borders, and the deaths of migrants will dissuade others from making the same trip. The Midlands Revolt failed, but the effect of migrants' refusal to abide by the global border regime is still an open question.

French philosophers Gilles Deleuze and Felix Guattari note that "history is always written from the sedentary point of view and in the name of a unitary State apparatus, at least a possible one, even when the topic is nomads. What is lacking is a Nomadology, the opposite of history."[37] They contrast the ordering logic of the state with the nomad, who is continuously en route, whose trip does not have a beginning and an endpoint but is always in the middle. They argue that movement should constitute an alternative approach to understanding the human condition that does not privilege the sedentary state. Michel de Certeau, author of *The Practice of Everyday Life*, acknowledges the extent that the ordering project of the state has come to dominate life to the point that it is difficult to act outside of it, but his contribution is the notion of the tactic, the little actions by individuals that work to subvert the order of the state.[38] De Certeau uses the example of a pedestrian moving through a city to explain how the order of the city is abided by and refused, through seemingly minor decisions that accumulate to signify a larger challenge to authority.

Refusing to abide by these enclosures and movement restrictions is a political act that can expose the violence of borders and the inequality of the global border regime. For much of the twentieth century, borders and state sovereignty were depoliticized in the sense that they were not up for debate.[39] It was taken for granted that humans lived in states, those states contained nations, and those nations should be the fundamental political units in the world. This idea drove the Treaty of Versailles at the end of World War I and is the foundation of the post–World War II world organized through the United Nations. The movements of migrants are tactics that repoliticize the concepts of states, borders, and nations. This repoliticization does not necessarily mean the concepts are rejected; it could result in a further hardening of borders and more extreme systems of migrant capture and control, as the xenophobic responses in many countries attest.

Nevertheless, the thousands of deaths at borders and the callous and inhumane treatment of migrants create an opening to question the underlying logic of the state system that is predicated on violent exclusion at borders. Despite the deaths at borders and the violence of the state, millions more people continue to move. These migrants' decisions are what Simon Springer terms a "'revolution of the everyday' where individuals become 'insurgents' by refusing the existing structures of domination and walking their own way."[40] By refusing to abide by a wall, map, property line, border, identity document, or legal regime, mobile people upset the state's schemes of exclusion, control, and violence. They do this simply by moving.

Notes

Introduction

1. In this book, I use the general term *migrant* to refer to anyone who is moving from one place to another. The term *refugee* is more limited and is defined by the 1951 United Nations Convention on Refugees as someone who has fled across a border due to political persecution in their home country. Chapter 1 includes a discussion of the usage and limits of migrant and refugee.
2. United Nations High Commissioner for Refugees, *World at War*, Geneva: United Nations High Commissioner for Refugees, 2015.
3. T. Brian and F. Laczko, *Fatal Journeys: Tracking Lives Lost during Migration*, Geneva: International Organization for Migration, 2014.
4. P. Pallister-Wilkins, "The Humanitarian Policing of 'Our Sea,'" *Border Criminologies*, http://bordercriminologies.law.ox.ac.uk, 2015; J. Stevens, *States without Nations: Citizenship for Mortals*, New York: Columbia University Press, 2011; H. Walia, *Undoing Border Imperialism*, Oakland, CA: AK Press, 2013.
5. In this book, I use the general terms *state* and *rulers*. I am aware that these are simplifications and that states are made up of multiple individuals who collectively create and reproduce the practices of the state. The state is not a monolithic entity but a collection of organizations and individuals. However, for the purposes of this analysis, *state* is a useful term to indicate a general set of practices over a long historical period.
6. L. Benton, *A Search for Sovereignty: Law and Geography in European Empires 1400–1900*, Cambridge, UK: Cambridge University Press, 2010; J. C. Scott, *Seeing Like a State: How Certain Schemes to Improve the Condition Have Failed*, New Haven, CT: Yale University Press, 1998; M. Foucault, "Governmentality," in P. Rabinow and N. Rose, eds., *The Essential Foucault: Selections from Essential Works of Foucault, 1954–1984*, New York: New Press, 2003, 229–45.

7. J. Forde-Johnston, *Hadrian's Wall*, London: M. Joseph, 1977; J. Lovell, *The Great Wall: China against the World, 1000 BC–2000 AD*, New York: Grove Press, 2006; C. Rojas, *The Great Wall: A Cultural History*, Cambridge, MA: Harvard University Press, 2010; B. Sterling, *Do Good Fences Make Good Neighbors? What History Teaches Us about Strategic Barriers and International Security*, Washington, DC: Georgetown University Press, 2009; A. Waldron, *The Great Wall: From History to Myth*, Cambridge, UK: Cambridge University Press, 1989.

8. This book relies on several primary research methods. The first is field research at borders and surrounding areas. Field research involves interviews with people moving through borders, residents of border areas, and officials involved in the management of borders; participant observation in the form of crossing borders and walking along boundary lines; and documentation of security practices at borders through the observation of security personnel and the infrastructure of the border. Because many of the individuals interviewed for the book are in vulnerable situations, pseudonyms are used for some to protect their identity. When a pseudonym is used, it is indicated with a footnote. The book draws on fieldwork conducted in Bangladesh and India from August 2006 until April 2007, in Israel and Palestine from May until July 2010, in Texas and New Mexico in March 2011, in California in March 2013, in England in May 2014, and in Morocco and the European Union on several different occasions from August 2014 until July 2015. This field research was supported by the US National Science Foundation under Grant No. 0602206, the American Institute of Bangladesh Studies, the Political Geography Specialty Group of the American Association of Geographers, and the Department of Geography at the University of Hawai'i. Language is often a challenge when conducting field research. In addition to English, I speak Bengali and Spanish with proficiency but not necessarily complete fluency. In India, Bangladesh, Palestine, and Morocco I worked with local guides and translators who assisted with logistics and interpreted conversations. In Spain and at the US–Mexico border, I interpreted Spanish conversations. Working with a research assistant is beneficial because they can provide local knowledge to help navigate unfamiliar customs and practices. They can also quickly explain what the research is about. However, research assistants also inevitably filter the data by putting it into their own words and framing the interactions with interview subjects. While recognizing these limitations, I benefited immensely from all of the work of my research

assistants. In addition to field research, this book relies on the analysis of government documents, reports, and speeches by officials. These reports are critical for understanding the extent of changes to borders, how they are funded, and how these changes are represented by those making the decisions.

9. E. Balibar, *Violence and Civility: On the Limits of Political Philosophy,* New York: Columbia University Press, 2015; S. Carrol, ed., *Cultures of Violence: Interpersonal Violence in Historical Perspective,* New York: Palgrave Macmillan, 2007; N. Peluso and M. Watts, *Violent Environments,* Ithaca, NY: Cornell University Press, 2001; J. Tyner and J. Inwood, "Violence as Fetish: Geography, Marxism, and Dialectics," *Progress in Human Geography* 38, 2014, 771–85.

10. Violence Prevention Alliance, http://www.who.int/violence prevention/approach/definition/en.

11. J. Galtung, "Violence, Peace, and Peace Research," *Journal of Peace Research* 6, 1969: 167–91, 170–1.

12. Tyner and Inwood, "Violence as Fetish."

1. The European Union: The World's Deadliest Border

1. H. De Haas, "The Myth of Invasion: The Inconvenient Realities of African Migration to Europe," *Third World Quarterly* 7, 2008, 1305–22; X. Ferrer-Gallardo, "Territorial (Dis)continuity Dynamics between Ceuta and Morocco: Conflictual Fortification vis-à-vis Co-operation Interaction at the EU Border in Africa," *Tijdschrift voor Economische en Sociale Geografie* 102, 2011, 24–38; X. Ferrer-Gallardo and A. Albet-Mas, "EU-Limboscapes: Ceuta and the Proliferation of Migrant Detention Spaces across the European Union," *European Urban and Regional Studies,* 2013; P. Gold, *Europe or Africa? A Contemporary Study of the Spanish North African Enclaves of Ceuta and Melilla,* Liverpool: Liverpool University Press, 2000; C. González, "Ceuta and Melilla: Clouds over the African Spanish Towns: Muslim Minorities, Spaniards' Fears and Morocco–Spain Mutual Dependence," *Journal of North African Studies* 12, 2007, 219–34; T. López-Guzmán, V. Gonzàlez Fernàndez, L. Herrera Torres, and O. Lorenzo Quiles, "Melilla: Ciudad Fronteriza Internacional e Intercontinental," *Frontera Norte* 19, 2007, 7–35; C. Mutlu and C. Leite, "Dark Side of the Rock: Borders, Exceptionalism and the Precarious Case of Ceuta and Melilla," *Eurasian Border Review* 3, 2012, 21–39.

2. These are pseudonyms because the situation for migrants in Morocco, and at many other borders described in this book, is dangerous. Anonymity was granted to most interviewees in order to allow them to speak freely without fear of reprisals from border guards or officials.

3. Brian and Laczko, *Fatal Journeys*, 2014.

4. European Union Agency for Fundamental Rights, "Treatment of Third-Country Nationals at the EU's External Borders: Protecting Fundamental Rights at the EU Sea Borders," n.d., http://fra .europa.eu.

5. For a critique of this narrative, see J. Agnew, *Globalization and Sovereignty*, Lanham, MD: Rowman & Littlefield, 2009; A. Paasi, "Boundaries as Social Processes: Territoriality in a World of Flows," *Geopolitics* 3, 1998, 69–88; A. Paasi, "Bounded Spaces in a Borderless World: Border Studies, Power, and the Autonomy of Territory," *Journal of Power* 2, 2009, 213–34.

6. E. Balibar, "Europe as Borderland," *Environment and Planning D: Society and Space*, 2009, vol. 27, 190–215; G. Popescu, *Bordering and Ordering the Twenty-First Century: Understanding Borders*, Lanham, MD: Rowman & Littlefield, 2012; T. Raeymaekers, "Introduction: Europe's Bleeding Border and the Mediterranean as a Relational Space," *ACME* 13, 2014, 163–72.

7. Frontex, "Governance Documents," 2014, www.frontex.europa. edu; H. van Houtum and R. Pijpers, "The European Union as a Gated Community: The Two-Faced Border and Immigration Regime of the EU," *Antipode* 39, 2007, 291–309; N. Vaughan-Williams, "Borderwork Beyond Inside/Outside? Frontex, the Citizen-Detective and the War on Terror," *Space & Polity* 12, 2008, 63–79.

8. Van Houtum and Pijpers, "European Union as a Gated Community"; H. van Houtum, "Human Blacklisting: The Global Apartheid of the EU's External Border Regime," *Environment and Planning D: Society and Space* 28, 2010, 957–76.

9. I. Ibba and B. Molinario, "Eritrean Survivor of Lampedusa Tragedy Returns to Honor the Dead, Meet Pope Francis," Rome: United Nations High Commissioner for Refugees, 2014.

10. United Nations High Commissioner for Refugees, *World at War*, 2015.

11. United Nations Commission of Inquiry on Human Rights in Eritrea, 2015.

12. Art. 1.A.2 of the 1951 *Convention Relating to the Status of Refugees*.

13. Eurostat, "Asylum Statistics," n.d., http://ec.europa.eu.

14. I. Kershner, "Netanyahu Rejects Calls for Israel to Accept Syrian Refugees," *New York Times,* September 6, 2015.

15. L. Bialasiewicz, "Borders, Above All?" *Political Geography* 30, 2011, 299–300; L. Bialasiewicz, "Off-shoring and Out-sourcing the Borders of EUrope: Libya and EU Border Work in the Mediterranean, *Geopolitics* 17, 2012, 843–66; M. Collyer and R. King, "Producing Transnational Space: International Migration and the Extra-territorial Reach of State Power," *Progress in Human Geography* 39, 2015, 185–204.

16. The Interactive Map on Migration, an integrated map that shows the shifting routes of migration, can be viewed at http://www.imap-migration.org.

17. International Organization for Migration, "Mediterranean Migrant Arrivals in 2016," iom.int, March 8, 2016.

18. Associated Press, "No Passage for Afghans on Balkan Route into Western Europe," February 26, 2016.

19. C. Heller, L. Pezzani, and Situ Studio, "Report on the 'Left-to-Die Boat,'" www.forensic-architecture.org, 2012.

20. E. Gayle, "Greece's Illegal Push Backs of Asylum Boats Puts Lives at Risk, Says Amnesty International," *Euronews,* August 25, 2015.

21. A. Travis, "UK Axes Support for Mediterranean Migrant Rescue Plan," *Guardian*, October 7, 2014.

22. The full poem is reprinted in A. Zimet, "No One Leaves Home Unless Home Is the Mouth of a Shark," *Common Dreams*, September 4, 2015, commondreams.org/further/2015/09/04/no-one-leaves-home-unless-home-mouth-shark.

23. M. Renzi, "Helping Immigrants Is Everyone's Duty," *New York Times*, April 23, 2015.

24. Raeymaekers, "Introduction," 165.

25. Brian and Laczko, *Fatal Journeys*, 88.

26. J. Carling, "Migration Control and Migrant Fatalities at the Spanish–African Borders," *International Migration Review* 41, 2007, 316–43. S. Grant, "Recording and Identifying European Frontier Deaths," *European Journal of Migration and Law* 13, 2011, 135–56; Spijkerboer, "Human Costs of Border Control."

27. Brian and Laczko, *Fatal Journeys*.

28. P. Pallister-Wilkins, "Humanitarian Policing of 'Our Sea.'"

2. The US–Mexico Border: Rise of a Militarized Zone

1. This is a pseudonym. She requested anonymity because she regularly crosses the bridge and interacts with CBP officials.

2. D. Lutterbeck, "Between Police and Military: The New Security Agenda and the Rise of Gendarmeries," *Cooperation and Conflict* 39, 2004, 45–68; D. Lutterbeck, "Policing Migration in the Mediterranean," *Mediterranean Politics* 11, 2006, 59–82. M. Manrique Gil, J. Barna, P. Hakala, B. Rey, and E. Claros, *Mediterranean Flows into Europe: Migration and the EU's Foreign Policy In-Depth Analysis*, Strasbourg: Directorate-General for External Policies, European Parliament, 2014.

3. There are a number of excellent books on the history of the US–Mexico border. See, for example, P. Andreas, *Border Games: Policing the US–Mexico Divide*, Ithaca: Cornell University Press, 2009; M. Dear, *Why Walls Won't Work: Repairing the US-Mexico Divide*, Oxford: Oxford University Press, 2013; J. Nevins, *Operation Gatekeeper and Beyond: The War on "Illegals" and the Remaking of the US–Mexico Boundary*, New York: Routledge, 2010; T. Payan, *Three US–Mexico Border Wars: Drugs, Immigration, and Homeland Security*, Westport, CT: Praeger Security, 2006.

4. Two recent books have begun to focus on the history and current militarization of the Border Patrol: K. L. Hernandez, *Migra! A History of the US Border Patrol*, Berkeley: University of California Press, 2010; T. Miller, *Border Patrol Nation: Dispatches from the Front Lines of Border Security*, San Francisco: City Lights Books, 2014.

5. Tim Dunn and Joe Heyman's work illustrates the effect of these changes to policy. T. Dunn, *The Militarization of the U.S.–Mexico Border, 1978–1992: Low-Intensity Conflict Doctrine Comes Home*, Austin, TX: CMAS Books, 1996; T. Dunn, "Border Militarization via Drug and Immigration Enforcement: Human Rights Implications," *Social Justice* 28, 2001, 7–30; T. Dunn, *Blockading the Border and Human Rights: The El Paso Operation That Remade Immigration Enforcement*, Austin: University of Texas Press, 2009; J. Heyman, "State Effects on Labor Exploitation: The INS and Undocumented Immigrants at the Mexico–United States Border," *Critique of Anthropology* 18, 1998, 157–80; J. Heyman, "Why Interdiction? Immigration Law Enforcement at the United States–Mexico Border," *Regional Studies* 33, 1999, 619–30; J. Heyman, "Constructing a Virtual Wall: Race and Citizenship in US–Mexico Border Policing," *Journal of the Southwest*

50, 2008, 305–34; J. Heyman, "Trust, Privilege, and Discretion in the Governance of the US Borderlands with Mexico," *Canadian Journal of Law and Society* 24, 2009, 367–90; J. Heyman and J. Ackleson, "United States Border Security after 9/11," in J. Winterdyk and K. Sundberg, eds., *Border Security in the al-Qaeda Era,* New York: CRC Press, 2009, 37–75; J. Heyman and H. Campbell, "The Militarization of the United States–Mexico Border Region," *Revista de Estudos Universitários* (Universidade de Sorocaba, Brazil) 38, 2012, 75–94.

6. Data from the US Customs and Border Protection website: cbp. gov.

7. C. Johnson, "Former Border Protection Insider Alleges Corruption, Distortion in Agency," *National Public Radio,* August 28, 2014.

8. D. Meissner, D. Kerwin, M. Chishti, and C. Bergeron, *Immigration Enforcement in the United States: The Rise of a Formidable Machinery,* Washington, DC: Migration Policy Institute, 2013.

9. Vision Gain, *Global Border Security Market 2013–2023: UAVs, UGVs, and Perimeter Surveillance Systems,* 2013; R. Abrahamsen and M. Williams, *Security Beyond the State: Private Security in International Politics,* Cambridge, UK: Cambridge University Press, 2011.

10. Miller, *Border Patrol Nation*; L. Martin, "'Catch and Remove': Detention, Deterrence, and Discipline in US Noncitizen Family Detention Practice," *Geopolitics* 17, 2012, 312–34.

11. United States Conference of Catholic Bishops, *Unlocking Human Dignity: A Plan to Transform the U.S. Immigration Detention System,* Washington, DC: United States Conference of Catholic Bishops and Center for Migration Studies, 2015, 7.

12. The increase in formal deportations is due to the change in Border Patrol policy. If voluntary removals from previous decades were included, the increase would not be as steep. Nevertheless, the formalization of the process of deportations has significant impacts on the immigrants who have a record and who face more serious consequences if they are caught again.

13. G. Bridge, "Territory, now in 3D!" *Political Geography* 34, 2013, 55–7; S. Elden, "Secure the Volume: Vertical Geopolitics and the Depth of Power," *Political Geography* 34, 2013, 35–51; P. Power, *The New Wild West: Military Support in Border Security Operations,* MA thesis, Fort Leavenworth, KS: US Army Command and General Staff College, 2012; C. Sorrensen, "Making the Subterranean Visible: Security, Tunnels, and the United States–Mexico Border," *Geographical Review* 104, 2014, 328–45.

14. US Secure Fence Act, 2006, http://www.gpo.gov/fdsys/pkg/PLAW-109publ367/html/PLAW-109publ367.htm.

15. D. Bigo, "Freedom and Speed in Enlarged Borderzones," in V. Squire, ed., *The Contested Politics of Mobility: Borderzones and Irregularity*, New York: Routledge, 2011; D. Bigo, "The (In)securitization Practices of the Three Universes of EU Border Control: Military/Navy—Border Guards/Police—Database Analysts," *Security Dialogue* 45, 2014, 209–25; A. Diener and J. Hagen, *Borders: A Very Short Introduction*, Oxford: Oxford University Press, 2012; Neocleous, *War Power, Police Power*.

16. T. Weiss, "The Blurring Border between the Police and the Military: A Debate without Foundations," *Cooperation and Conflict* 46, 2011, 396–405.

17. Neocleous, *War Power, Police Power*, 14.

18. P. Kraska, "Militarization and Policing—Its Relevance to 21st-Century Police," *Policing* 1, 2007, 501.

19. P. Kraska, ed., *Militarizing the American Criminal Justice System: The Changing Roles of the Armed Forces and the Police*, Boston: Northeastern University Press, 2001, 501.

20. Heyman and Campbell, "Militarization of the United States–Mexico Border Region."

21. Kraska, "Militarization and Policing," 503.

22. Ibid.

23. S. Musgrave, T. Meagher, and G. Dance, "The Pentagon Finally Details Its Weapons-for-Cops Giveaway," *Marshall Project*, December 3, 2014, https://www.themarshallproject.org.

24. Kraska, "Militarization and Policing," 2007.

25. Miller, *Border Patrol Nation*.

26. Posse Comitatus Act, 1878, 18 U.S.C. § 1385, 20 Stat. 152.

27. C. Haddal, *Border Security: The Role of the Border Patrol*, Washington, DC: Congressional Research Services, 2010; Hernandez, *Migra!*

28. J. Scahill, *Dirty Wars: The World is a Battlefield*, New York: Nation Books, 2013.

29. B. Lepore, "Border Security: Observations on Costs, Benefits, and Challenges of a Department of Defense Role in Helping to Secure the Southwest Land Border," highlights of GAO-12-657T, a testimony before the Subcommittee on Border and Maritime Security, House Committee on Homeland Security, Washington, DC: US Government Accountability Office, 2012.

30. R. Mason, *Securing America's Borders: The Role of the Military*, Washington, DC: Congressional Research Service, 2013.

31. P. Brownell, "Border Militarization and the Reproduction of

Mexican Migrant Labor," *Social Justice* 28, 2001, 69–92; T. Dunn, "Border Militarization via Drug and Immigration Enforcement: Human Rights Implications," *Social Justice* 28, 2001, 7–30.

32. Lepore, "Border Security."

33. A. Isacson and M. Meyer, *Beyond the Border Buildup: Security and Migrants along the U.S.–Mexico Border*, Washington, DC: Washington Office on Latin America, 2012.

34. B. Pollachek, "Northern Command Helps Border Patrol with Southwest Mission," *United States Army News*, January 30, 2012. http://www.army.mil/article/72606.

35. Ibid.

36. T. Miller, "Strykers on the Border," North American Committee on South America, 2012, https://nacla.org/.

37. Johnson, "Former Border Protection Insider Alleges Corruption."

38. Ibid.

39. D. Martínez, G. Cantor, and W. Ewing, *No Action Taken: Lack of CBP Accountability in Responding to Complaints of Abuse*, Washington, DC: American Immigration Council, 2014.

40. Johnson, "Former Border Protection Insider Alleges Corruption."

41. United States Border Patrol, *Use of Force Policy, Guidelines, and Procedure Handbook*, Washington, DC: Border Patrol Office of Training and Development, 2014.

42. K. McGill, "Appeals Court: Family of Teen Shot in Mexico by US Border Patrol Agent Cannot Sue in US Court," *US News and World Report*, April 24, 2015.

43. US Department of Justice, National Drug Intelligence Center, *National Drug Threat Assessment 2009*, 3; C. Haddal, Y. Kim, and M. Garcia, *Border Security: Barriers along the US International Border*, Washington, DC: Congressional Research Services, 2010.

44. Brian and Laczko, *Fatal Journeys*, 25, quoting an Amnesty International report.

45. Instituto para las Mujeres in la Migracion, *2013 Annual Report*, 2013, http://www.imumi.org/; Comision Nacional de los Derechos Humanos, www.cndh.org.mx.

46. Brian and Laczko, *Fatal Journeys*; M. Jimenez, *Humanitarian Crisis: Migrant Deaths at the US–Mexico Border*, San Diego: American Civil Liberties Union, 2009; J. Loyd, M. Mitchelson, and A. Burridge, *Beyond Walls and Cages: Prisons, Borders, and Global Crisis*, Athens: University of Georgia Press, 2012; T. Spijkerboer, "The Human Costs of Border Control," *European Journal of Migration and Law* 9, 2007, 127–39; J. Williams and G. Boyce, "Fear, Loathing and the Everyday Geopolitics of

Encounter in the Arizona Borderlands," *Geopolitics* 18, 2013, 895–916.

47. US Customs and Border Protection, *National Border Patrol Strategy,* Washington, DC: US Border Patrol, 2005.

48. B. Anderson and B. Parks, "Symposium on Border Crossing Deaths: Introduction," *Journal of Forensic Sciences* 53, 2008, 6–7.

49. L. Urrea, *The Devil's Highway: A True Story,* New York: Little, Brown, 2004.

50. L. Weber and S. Pickering, *Globalization and Borders: Death at the Frontier,* London: Palgrave Macmillan, 2011.

3. The Global Border Regime

1. Both videos are on YouTube. The crane video is titled "TITO BILIN 26-06-2008," March 27, 2008; the shooting, "VIDEO Soldado israelí dispara a palestino vendado y esposado," July 21, 2008.

2. M. Frykberg, "Palestinian 'Che' Blindfolded and Shot," Inter Press Service, July 25, 2008.

3. The video of the protest is on YouTube, "The Shooting of Bassem Abu Rahmah," January 25, 2010.

4. Jewish Telegraphic Agency, "Netanyahu 'Declaring War' on Rock Throwers Following Motorist's Death," September 16, 2015.

5. M. Van Reisen, M. Estefanos, and C. Rijken, *Human Trafficking in the Sinai: Refugees between Life and Death,* Oisterwijk, Netherlands: Wolf Legal Publishers, 2012.

6. J. Halper, *Obstacles to Peace: A Reframing of the Israeli-Palestinian Conflict,* Jerusalem: ICAHD, 2009.

7. Popular Struggle Organizing Committee, "Bil'in Grassroots Leader Mohammed Khatib Arrested in Late-Night Raid," *Electronic Intifada,* January 28, 2010.

8. H. Sherwood, "Israeli Military and Palestinians Clash over Death of West Bank Woman," *Guardian,* January 6, 2011.

9. H. Greenberg, "Did Palestinians Lie about Protestor's Death?" *Ynet,* January 4, 2011.

10. Bangladesh government data. The Bangladeshi NGO Odhikar maintains a database on their website of killings at the border, Odhikar.com. Additional information is available in *"Trigger Happy": Excessive Use of Force by Indian Troops at the Bangladesh Border,* New York: Human Rights Watch, 2010.

11. *Economist,* "Felani's Last Steps," February 3, 2011.

12. W. Van Schendel, *A History of Bangladesh*, Cambridge, UK: Cambridge University Press, 2009.

13. W. Van Schendel, *The Bengal Borderland: Beyond State and Nation in South Asia*, London: Anthem Press, 2005.

14. J. Chatterji, *Bengal Divided*, Cambridge, UK: Cambridge University Press, 1994; L. Chester, "Boundary Commissions as Tools to Safeguard British Interests at the End of Empire," *Journal of Historical Geography* 34, 2008, 494–515; J. Cons, "Histories of Belonging(s): Narrating Territory, Possession, and Dispossession at the India–Bangladesh Border," *Modern Asian Studies* 46, 2012, 527–58; J. Cons, "Narrating Boundaries: Framing and Contesting Suffering, Community, and Belonging in Enclaves along the India–Bangladesh Border," *Political Geography* 35, 2013, 37–46; J. Cons and R. Sanyal, "Geographies at the Margin: Borders in South Asia, an Introduction," *Political Geography* 35, 2013, 5–13; H. Shewly, "Abandoned Spaces and Bare Life in the Enclaves of the India–Bangladesh Border," *Political Geography* 32, 2013, 23–31; M. Sur, "Bamboo Baskets and Barricades: Gendered Landscapes at the India–Bangladesh Border," in B. Kalir and M. Sur, eds., *Transnational Flows and Permissive Polities: Ethnographies of Human Mobilities in Asia*, Amsterdam: IIAS Publications, 2013, 127–50; V. Zamindar, *The Long Partition and the Making of Modern South Asia: Refugees, Boundaries, Histories*, New York: Columbia University Press, 2007.

15. *Bdnews24*, "Delhi Plans to Seal India–Bangladesh Border to Check Illegal Migration," August 11, 2015, bdnews24.com.

16. E. Kabir, *Border Fencing: A Major Irritant in Indo-Bangla Relations*, Dhaka: News Network, 2005.

17. *Financial Express Bangladesh*, "Accused BSF Man Acquitted," September 7, 2013, thefinancialexpress-bd.com.

18. Human Rights Watch, *"All You Can Do Is Pray": Crimes against Humanity and Ethnic Cleansing of Rohingya Muslims in Burma's Arakan State*, New York: Human Rights Watch, 2013.

19. Human Rights Watch, *Burmese Refugees in Bangladesh: Still No Durable Solutions*, New York: Human Rights Watch, 2000.

20. S. Miglani, "Rohingya Huddled in Bangladesh Camps Fear Plan to Move Them On," Reuters, June 2, 2015.

21. Human Rights Watch, *"All You Can Do Is Pray,"* 59.

22. A. Lindblom, E. Marsh, T. Motala, K. Munyan, "Persecution of the Rohingya Muslims: Is Genocide Occurring in Myanmar's Rakhine State? A Legal Analysis," New Haven, CT: Allard K. Lowenstein International Human Rights Clinic, Yale Law School, 2015.

23. United Nations High Commissioner for Refugees, *South-East Asia: Irregular Maritime Movements, January–March 2015*, www.unhcr.com, 2015.

24. T. Fuller and J. Cochrane, "Rohingya Migrants from Myanmar, Shunned by Malaysia, Are Spotted Adrift in Andaman Sea," *New York Times*, May 14, 2015.

25. C. Stewart and S. Balogh, "Boatpeople 'Labourers' Not Rohingya: Indonesia," *Australian*, May 23, 2015.

26. L. Mogelson, "The Dream Boat," *The New York Times Magazine*, November 15, 2013.

27. Australian Border Deaths Database, http://artsonline.monash .edu.au/thebordercrossingobservatory/publications/australian-border-deaths-database.

28. Australian Department of Immigration and Border Protection, "Counter People Smuggling Communication," n.d., http://www .customs.gov.au/site/offshore-communication-campaign-people-smuggling.asp.

29. K. Coddington and A. Mountz, "Countering Isolation with Use of Technology: How Asylum-Seeking Detainees on Islands in the Indian Ocean Use Social Media to Transcend Their Confinement," *Journal of the Indian Ocean Region* 10, 2014, 97–112.

30. B. Doherty, "Australia's Offshore Detention Damages Asylum Seekers Because It's Supposed To," *Guardian*, January 18, 2016.

31. This is not to say that power is only held by the state or that the borders of states contain power. Instead, the point is that power to control resources and movement is organized through the state. For a critique of assuming a bounded state, see J. Agnew, "The Territorial Trap: The Geographical Assumptions of International Relations Theory," *Review of International Political Economy* 1, 1994, 53–80.

32. Brown, *Walled States*; M. Stephenson and L. Zanotti, eds., *Building Walls and Dissolving Borders*, Aldershot, UK: Ashgate, 2013.

33. Brown, *Walled States*, 24.

34. J. Barkan, *Corporate Sovereignty*, Minneapolis: University of Minnesota Press, 2013; S. Sassen, *Territory, Authority, Rights: From Medieval to Global Assemblages*, Princeton, NJ: Princeton University Press, 2006.

35. S. Wright, "Policing Borders in a Time of Rapid Climate Change," in J. Scheffran, M. Brzoska, H. Brauch, P. Link, and J. Schilling, eds., *Climate Change, Human Security and Violent Conflict: Challenges for Societal Stability*, Berlin: Springer, 2012, 351–70.

36. This idea was first suggested to me by Matthew Longo. See M.

Longo, "A '21st Century Border'? Cooperative Border Controls in the US and EU after 9/11," *Journal of Borderlands Studies* (forthcoming).

4. The Global Poor

1. D. Nasaw, *Andrew Carnegie*, New York: Penguin Books, 2006.
2. C. Wills, *Destination America*, London: Dorling Kindersley, 2005.
3. Data from Australian Migration Heritage Center, migrationheritage .nsw.gov.au/homepage.
4. Ibid., 42.
5. M. Davis, "Planet of Slums," *New Left Review* 26, 2004, 5–31.
6. R. Peet, *Unholy Trinity: The IMF, the World Bank, and the WTO*, 2nd ed., London: Zed Books, 2009.
7. Mongabay.com, "Population Estimates for Lagos, Nigeria, 1950– 2015," n.d., http://books.mongabay.com/population_estimates/ full/Lagos-Nigeria.html.
8. D. Forsyth, *Encyclopedia of Human Rights*, Vol. 1, Oxford: Oxford University Press, 2009, 399.
9. T. Cresswell, *On the Move: Mobility in the Modern Western World*, London: Routledge, 2006.
10. W. Quigley, "Five Hundred Years of English Poor Laws, 1349– 1834: Regulating the Working and Non-working Poor," *Akron Law Review* 30, 1996, 73–128.
11. P. Linebaugh, *The Magna Carta Manifesto: Liberties and Commons for All*, Berkeley: University of California Press, 2008.
12. An English translation of the Magna Carta is available here: http://www.bl.uk/magna-carta/articles/magna-carta-english- translation#sthash.VYMxMt5r.dpuf.
13. J. Torpey, *The Invention of the Passport: Surveillance, Citizenship, and the State*, Cambridge, UK: Cambridge University Press, 2000.
14. Quigley, *Five Hundred Years*; W. Trattner, *From Poor Law to Welfare State: A History of Social Welfare in the United States*, 6th ed., New York: Simon & Schuster, 2007.
15. B. Anderson, *Us and Them: The Dangerous Politics of Immigra- tion Controls*, Oxford: Oxford University Press, 2013.
16. D. Blackmon, *Slavery by Another Name: The Re-enslavement of Black Americans from the Civil War to World War II*, New York: Doubleday, 2009.
17. S. Elden, "Leibniz and Geography: Geologist, Paleontologist, Biologist, Historian, Political Theorist, and Geopolitician,"

Geographica Helvetica 68, 2013, 81–93; A. Murphy, "The Sovereign State System as Political-Territorial Ideal: Historical and Contemporary Considerations," in T. Biersteker and C. Weber, eds., *State Sovereignty as Social Construct,* Cambridge, UK: Cambridge University Press, 1996, 81–120.

18. M. Foucault, "The Subject and Power," *Critical Inquiry* 8, 1982, 777–95, 777.

19. Scott, *Seeing Like a State.*

20. Foucault, "Governmentality," 244.

21. R. Bellamy, *Citizenship: A Very Short Introduction,* Oxford: Oxford University Press, 2008.

22. Ibid., 35.

23. J. Rousseau, *Of the Social Contract, or Principles of Political Right,* Paris, 1762.

24. T. Hobbes, *Leviathan,* London, 1651; J. Locke, *Two Treaties on Government,* London: Awnsham Churchill, 1689.

25. M. Caritat, Marquis de Condorcet, "The First Essay on the Political Rights of Women, A Translation of Condorcet's Essay Sur l'admission des femmes aux droits de Cité (On the Admission of Women to the Rights of Citizenship)," trans. by A. Vickery, Letchworth, UK: Garden City Press, 1912.

26. Declaration of the Rights of Man and Citizen, 1789.

27. The institution of the House of Representatives in the United States did create one venue for the general public to participate in decision-making.

28. R. Brubaker, "The Manichean Myth: Rethinking the Distinction Between 'Civic' and 'Ethnic' Nationalism," in H. Kriesi, ed., *Nation and National Identity: The European Experience in Perspective,* Zurich: Ruegger, 1999, 55–71.

29. Torpey, *Invention of the Passport,* 1–2.

30. Ibid., 93.

31. B. Anderson, *Imagined Communities: Reflections on the Origin and Spread of Nationalism,* 2nd ed., London: Verso, 1991.

32. Torpey, *Invention of the Passport,* 97.

33. M. Salter, "The Global Visa Regime and the Political Technologies of the International Self: Borders, Bodies, Biopolitics," *Alternatives* 31, 2006, 167–89; M. Salter, *Politics at the Airport,* Minneapolis: University of Minnesota Press, 2008.

34. L. Amoore, "Biometric Borders: Governing Mobilities in the War on Terror," *Political Geography* 25, 2006, 336–51; L. Amoore, "Data Derivatives: On the Emergence of a Security Risk Calculus for Our Times," *Theory, Culture & Society* 28, 2011, 24–43; L. Amoore, *The Politics of Possibility: Risk and Security Beyond*

Probability, Durham, NC: Duke University Press, 2013; Popescu, *Bordering and Ordering,* 91–120.

35. R. Baldwin, P. Martin, and G. Ottaviano, "Global Income Divergence, Trade, and Industrialization: The Geography of Growth Take-offs," *Journal of Economic Growth* 6, 2001, 5–37.

36. V. Prashad, *The Darker Nations: A People's History of the Third World,* New York: New Press, 2007.

37. GDP per capita data from the World Bank, data.worldbank.org.

38. S. Dalby, "Globalization or Global Apartheid? Boundaries and Knowledge in Postmodern Times," *Geopolitics* 3, 1998, pp. 132–50.

39. A.-L. Amilhat Szary, "Walls and Border Art: The Politics of Art Display," *Journal of Borderland Studies* 27, 2012, 213–28; W. Brown, *Walled States, Waning Sovereignty,* New York: Zone Books, 2010; M. Di Cintio, *Walls: Travels along the Barricades,* Berkeley, CA: Soft Skull Press, 2013; S. Rosière and R. Jones, "Teichopolitics: Re-considering Globalisation through the Role of Walls and Fences," *Geopolitics* 17, 2012, 217–34; K. Till, J. Sundberg, W. Pullan, C. Psaltis, C. Makriyianni, R. Zincir Celal, M. Samani, and L. Dowler, "Interventions in the Political Geographies of Walls," *Political Geography* 33, 2013, 52–62.

5. Maps, Hedges, and Fences: Enclosing the Commons and Bounding the Seas

1. The historical material about the Midlands Revolt was gathered during a research trip to Northamptonshire in May 2014. Thanks to John Padwick for providing insights into the event and a trove of documents. John maintains a website that includes information on the revolt: J. Padwick, *Newton Rebels 1607,* http://www.newtonrebels.org.uk/rebels/academic.htm.

2. E. Gay, "The Midlands Revolt of 1607," *Transactions of the Royal Historical Society,* vol. 18, 1904, 195–244. Estimated populations of English counties in 1600 are available at http://www.visionof britain.org.uk/census/SRC_P/6/GB1841ABS_1.

3. Padwick, *Newton Rebels 1607.*

4. J.C. Scott, *The Art of Not Being Governed: An Anarchist History of Upland Southeast Asia,* New Haven, CT: Yale University Press, 2009.

5. Sterling, *Do Good Fences Make Good Neighbors?*

6. R. Jones, *Border Walls: Security and the War on Terror in the United States, India, and Israel,* London: Zed Books, 2012; Vallet, *Borders, Fences and Walls,* 1–10.

7. R. Sack, *Human Territoriality: Its Theory and Practice,* Cambridge, UK: Cambridge University Press, 1986, 19.

8. N. Blomley, "Law, Property and the Geography of Violence: The Frontier, the Survey and the Grid," *Annals of the Association of American Geographers* 93, 2003, 121–41; N. Blomley, "Making Private Property: Enclosure, Common Right, and the Work of Hedges," *Rural History* 18, 2007, 1–21; N. Blomley, "Simplification Is Complicated: Property, Nature, and the River of Laws," *Environment and Planning A* 40, 2007, 1,825–42.

9. Scott, *Art of Not Being Governed,* 5.

10. E. Freyfogle, *On Private Property: Finding Common Ground on the Ownership of Land,* Boston: Beacon Press, 2007.

11. R. Gilman, "The Idea of Owning Land," *In Context* 8, 1984, 5–8.

12. E. Brown, "The Tyranny of a Construct: Feudalism and Historians of Medieval Europe," *American Historical Review* 79, 1974, 1,063–88; S. Reynolds, *Fiefs and Vassals: The Medieval Evidence Reinterpreted,* Oxford: Oxford University Press, 1994.

13. J. Yelling, *Common Field and Enclosure in England 1450–1850,* London: Macmillan, 1977.

14. H. Bradley, *The Enclosures in England: An Economic Reconstruction,* Ontario: Batoche Books, [1918] 2001.

15. H. Rothwell, ed., *English Historical Documents, Vol. 3, 1189–1327,* London: Eyre & Spottiswoode, 1975, 337–40.

16. R. Manning, *Village Revolts: Social Protest and Popular Disturbances in England, 1509–1640,* Oxford: Oxford University Press, 1988; Blomley, "Law, Property and the Geography of Violence"; Blomley, "Making Private Property"; Blomley, "Simplification Is Complicated."

17. Linebaugh, *Magna Carta Manifesto,* 48.

18. P. D. A. Harvey, *Maps in Tudor England,* Chicago: University of Chicago Press, 1993, 7.

19. J. B. Harley, *The New Nature of Maps,* P. Laxton, ed., Baltimore: Johns Hopkins Press, 2002.

20. J. B Harley and D. Woodward, *The History of Cartography,* vol. 1, Chicago: University of Chicago Press, 1987; Sack, *Human Territoriality;* T. Winichakul, *Siam Mapped: A History of the Geo-Body of a Nation,* Honolulu: University of Hawai'i Press, 1994; D. Wood, *The Power of Maps,* New York: Guilford Press, 1992.

21. Harvey, *Maps in Tudor England,* 1993, 15.

22. Ibid., 79.

23. R. Kain, J. Chapman, and R. Oliver, *The Enclosure Maps of England and Wales, 1595–1918,* Cambridge, UK: Cambridge University Press, 2004.

24. Harley, *New Nature of Maps*; Blomley, "Making Private Property."

25. Blomley, "Making Private Property," argues that material objects played an important role, like estate maps, in late sixteenth- and early seventeenth-century enclosure: "In particular, I emphasize the important work that hedges did, physically, symbolically and legally, in the dispossession of the commoner."

26. G. Monbiot, "A Land Reform Manifesto," February 22, 1995, http://www.monbiot.com/1995/02/22/a-land-reform-manifesto.

27. Gay, "Midlands Revolt," 233.

28. Manning, *Village Revolts*, 33; J. Wordie, "The Chronology of English Enclosure, 1500–1914," *Economic History Review* 36, 1983, 483–505. These figures are disputed, including by J. Chapman: see "Some Comments on Dr. Wordie's Calculation," *English History Review* 37, 1984, 557–9.

29. J. Neeson, *Commoners: Common Right, Enclosure and Social Change in England, 1700–1820*, Cambridge, UK: Cambridge University Press, 1993.

30. M. Turner, *English Parliamentary Enclosures*, Dawson, UK: Folkestone, 1980; J. Chapman, "The Extent and Nature of Parliamentary Enclosures," *Agricultural History Review* 35, 1987, 25–35.

31. E. P. Thompson, *The Making of the English Working Class*, New York: Pantheon, 1963, 217.

32. Blomley, "Law, Property, and the Geography of Violence," 127.

33. Manning, *Village Revolts*, 9.

34. M. Hardt and A. Negri, *Multitude: Ware and Democracy in the Age of Empire*, New York: Penguin, 2004, 202.

35. Freyfogle, *On Private Property*.

36. R. Netz, *Barbed Wire: An Ecological History of Modernity*, Middletown, CT: Wesleyan University Press, 2004.

37. There are many excellent books that delve into examples of this process. N. Dirks, "Guiltless Spoliation, Picturesque Beauty, Colonial Knowledge, and Colin Mackenzie's Survey of India," in C. Asher and T. Metcalf, eds., *Perceptions of South Asia's Visual Past*, New Delhi: American Institute of Indian Studies, 1994, 211–32; M. Edney, *Mapping an Empire: The Geographic Construction of British India 1765–1843*, Chicago: University of Chicago Press, 1997; T. Mitchell, *Colonising Egypt*, Cambridge, UK: Cambridge University Press, 1988; Winichakul, *Siam Mapped*.

38. J. Nevins and N. Peluso, eds., *Taking Southeast Asia to Market: Commodities, Nature, and People in Neoliberal Age*, Ithaca, NY: Cornell University Press, 2008.

39. D. Harvey, *The New Imperialism*, Oxford: Oxford University Press, 2003.

40. A. Jeffrey, C. McFarlane, and A. Vasudevan, "Rethinking Enclosure: Space, Subjectivity, and the Commons," *Antipode* 44, 2012, 1,247–67, 1,248.

41. S. Chavkin and M. Hudson, "New Investigation Reveals 3.4M Displaced by World Bank," *International Consortium of Investigative Journalists,* April 16, 2015.

42. C. Tilly, *Coercion, Capital, and European States, 990–1990 A.D.,* London: Basil Blackwell, 1990.

43. Winichakul, *Siam Mapped.*

44. G. Parker, ed., *The Thirty Years' War,* London: Routledge, 1997, 75.

45. Ibid., 193.

46. P. Wilson, *The Thirty Years' War: Europe's Tragedy,* Cambridge, MA: Harvard University Press, 2009, 753.

47. Elden, *Birth of Territory.*

48. Ibid., 312.

49. Wilson, *Thirty Years' War,* 754.

50. Parker, *Thirty Years' War,* 194.

51. P. Sahlins, *Boundaries: The Making of France and Spain in the Pyrenees,* Berkeley: University of California Press, 1989. This period "can hardly be summarized as the simple evolution from an empty zone to a precise line, but rather as the complex interplay of two notions of boundary—zonal and linear—and two ideas of sovereignty—jurisdictional and territorial" (7).

52. M. Foucault, "Governmentality"; M. Mann, *States, Wars and Capitalism: Studies in Political Sociology,* London: Basil Blackwell, 1988; Scott, *Seeing Like a State.*

53. Tilly, *Coercion, Capital, and European States.*

54. Quoted in J. Herbst, "The Creation and Maintenance of National Boundaries in Africa," *International Organization* 43, 1989, 673–92.

55. B. Heine and D. Nurse, eds., *African Languages: An Introduction,* Cambridge, UK: Cambridge University Press, 2000.

56. S. Pursley, "'Lines Drawn on an Empty Map': Iraq's Borders and the Legend of the Artificial State," *Jadaliyya,* June 2, 2015.

57. The Islamic State video can be found here: https://www.youtube.com/watch?v=i357G1HuFcI.

58. K. Dodds, "Flag Planting and Finger Pointing: The Law of the Sea, the Arctic, and the Political Geographies of the Outer Continental Shelf," *Political Geography* 29, 2010, 63–73; S. Lin and C. Schofield, "Lessons from the Bay of Bengal ITLOS Case: Stepping Offshore for a 'Deeper' Maritime Political Geography," *Geographical Journal* 180, 2014, 260–4; P. Steinberg, *The Social*

Construction of the Ocean, Cambridge, UK: Cambridge University Press, 2001.

59. B. Finney, "Myth, Experiment, and the Reinvention of Polynesian Voyaging," *American Anthropologist* 93, 1991, 383–404.

60. N. Bertz, *Diaspora and Nation in the Indian Ocean: Transnational Histories of Race and Urban Space in Tanzania*, Honolulu: University of Hawai'i Press, 2015; G. Hourani, *Arab Seafaring in the Indian Ocean in Ancient and Early Medieval Times*, Princeton, NJ: Princeton University Press, 1995.

61. D. Abulafia, *The Great Sea: A Human History of the Mediterranean*, Oxford: Oxford University Press, 2011.

62. Steinberg, *Social Construction of the Ocean*.

63. A copy of the proclamation is available here: http://www .presidency.ucsb.edu/ws/index.php?pid=12332.

64. B. Mansfield, "Neoliberalism in the Oceans: 'Rationalization,' Property Rights, and the Commons Question," in N. Heynen, J. McCarthy, S. Prudham, and P. Robbins, *Neoliberal Environments: False Promises and Unnatural Consequences*, New York: Routledge, 2007, 63–73.

65. United Nations, Convention on the Law of the Sea, 1982, http:// www.un.org/depts/los/convention_agreements/texts/unclos/ UNCLOS-TOC.htm.

66. Technically, these distances are measured from baselines. Baselines are generally the coast, but states can opt to use a straight baseline if they have many islands or a jagged coastline. Many states have opted for straight baselines because it often means they can claim more area as internal waters and consequently extend their EEZs farther out.

67. N. Parkins, "Staking a Claim: Deep-Sea Mining Nears Fruition," *Earth: The Science behind the Headlines*, May 24, 2014.

68. K. Dodds and M. Nuttal, *Scramble for the Poles? The Contemporary Geopolitics of the Arctic and Antarctic,* Cambridge, UK: Polity, 2015.

69. J. Robertson and B. Pierce, "90 Billion Barrels of Oil and 1,670 Trillion Cubic Feet of Natural Gas Assessed in the Arctic," Washington, DC: United States Geological Survey, 2008.

6. Bounding Wages, Goods, and Workers

1. Human Rights Watch, *"Whoever Raises Their Heads Suffers Most"*: *Workers' Rights in Bangladesh's Garment Factories*, Washington, DC: Human Rights Watch, 2015.

2. The US revoked Bangladesh's special import relationship, but this is an imperfect solution because the result will be no jobs for many millions of poor Bangladeshis. On payments to Rana Plaza workers, see Clean Clothes Campaign, "Who Has Paid and Who Is Dragging Their Heels," May 2015, http://www.cleanclothes.org/ranaplaza/who-needs-to-pay-up.

3. Haznain Kaim, "Bangladeshi Seamstress: 'I Had No Choice but to Go to Work,'" *Der Spiegel*, May 16, 2013.

4. U. Sinclair, *The Jungle*, Urbana: University of Illinois Press, [1906] 1988, 124.

5. These included the Federal Meat Inspection Act of 1906 and the Pure Food and Drug Act of 1906.

6. T. Piketty, *Capital in the Twenty-First Century*, Cambridge, MA: Harvard University Press, 2014; F. Norris, "US Companies Thrive as Workers Fall Behind," *New York Times,* August 9, 2013.

7 J. M. Keynes, *The General Theory of Employment, Interest, and Money,* New York: Harcourt Brace, 1936.

8. F. Hayek, *The Road to Serfdom*, London: Routledge, 1944.

9. Picketty, *Capital.*

10. E. Rauchway, *A Very Short Introduction to the Great Depression and the New Deal,* Oxford: Oxford University Press, 2008.

11. Ibid.

12. J. Grossman, "Fair Labor Standards Act of 1938: Maximum Struggle for a Minimum Wage," *Monthly Labor Review,* June 1978, 22–30; Record of Discussion of FLSA of 1938, Washington, DC: U.S. Department of Labor, 38, 115, 124.

13. I. Berlin, *Personal Impressions,* Princeton, NJ: Princeton University Press, 2001.

14. Of course, the environmental implications of these decisions are clear now.

15. S. Marglin and J. Schor, eds., *The Golden Age of Capitalism: Reinterpreting the Postwar Experience,* Oxford: Clarendon Press, 1990.

16. Hayek, *Road to Serfdom,* 38–9.

17. US imports and exports as a percentage of GDP (nonadjusted). US Census Bureau (census.gov/foreign-trade/Press-Release/current_press_release/index.html) and US Commerce Department, Bureau of Economic Analysis (bea.gov/national/index.htm#gdp).

18. P. Dicken, *Global Shift: Mapping the Changing Contours of the World Economy,* New York: Guilford Press, 2015; D. Harvey, *The Condition of Postmodernity: An Inquiry into the Origins of Social Change*, Cambridge, UK: Blackwell, 1989; A. Lipietz, "Towards Global Fordism?" *New Left Review* 132, 1982, 33–7; A. Lipietz,

"New Tendencies in the International Division of Labor: Regimes of Accumulation and Modes of Regulation," in A. Scott, and M. Storper, eds., *Production, Work, and Territory: The Geographical Anatomy of Industrial Capitalism,* Boston: Allen & Unwin, 1986; E. Schoenberger, "From Fordism to Flexible Accumulation: Technology, Competitive Strategies, and International Locations," *Environment and Planning D: Society and Space* 6, 1988, 245–62.

19. Y. Monden, *Toyota Production System: An Integrated Approach to Just-in-Time,* 4th ed., Boca Raton, FL: CRC Press, 2007; Y. Sugimori, K. Kunsunoki, F. Cho, and S. Uchikawa, "Toyota Production System and Kanban System: Materialization of Just-in-Time and Respect-for-Human System," *International Journal of Production Research* 15, 1977, 546–53.

20. B. Sousa, "Regulating Japanese Automobile Imports: Some Implications of the Voluntary Quota System," *Boston College International and Comparative Law Review* 5, 1982, 431–60. Ward's Automotive (wardsauto.com) collects data on US automobile sales.

21. US imports and exports as a percentage of GDP (nonadjusted). Source: US Census Bureau and US Commerce Department, Bureau of Economic Analysis.

22. P. Andrews-Speed, R. Bleishwitz, T. Boersma, C. Johnson, G. Kemp, and S. Vandeveer, *Want, Waste or War? The Global Resource Nexus and the Struggle for Land, Energy, Food, Water, and Minerals,* New York: Earthscan, 2014; World Trade Organization, *World Trade Statistics,* Geneva: WTO, 2012.

23. Many geographers have written about this process. See, for example, N. Smith, *Uneven Development: Nature, Capital and the Production of Space,* Athens: University of Georgia Press, 1984.

24. Manufacturing employees and total employment data from the United States Federal Reserve, St. Louis. R. Scott, *The Manufacturing Footprint and the Importance of U.S. Manufacturing Jobs,* Washington, DC: Economic Policy Institute, 2015.

25. M. Villareal and I. Fergusson, *The North American Free Trade Agreement (NAFTA),* Washington, DC: Congressional Research Service, 2015.

26. R. Scott, "Heading South: US–Mexico Trade and Job Displacement after NAFTA," *Economic Policy Institute Briefing Paper,* 308, 2011.

27. Congressional Budget Office, *The Effects of NAFTA on US and Mexico Trade and GDP,* Washington, DC: Congressional Budget Office, 2003.

28. *Economist,* "The Arbitration Game," October 11, 2014.

29. Data from the United Nations Conference on Trade and Development, www.unctad.org.
30. L. Wallach, "NAFTA on Steroids," *Nation*, July 16, 2012.
31. *Economist*, "Playing Nicely," May 7, 2015.
32. D. Rosnick, *The Gains from Trade in the New Model from the IMF: Still Very Small*, Washington, DC: Center for Economic and Policy Research, 2015.
33. D. Harvey, *The Limits to Capital*, New York: Verso, 1982; Mezzadra and Neilson, *Border as Method*; Smith, *Uneven Development*.
34. The connection between economic change and migration is explored in: S. Sassen, *Expulsions: Brutality and Complexity in the Global Economy*, Cambridge, MA: Harvard University Press, 2014.
35. In addition to field research in Bangladesh in 2006 and 2007, I lived in rural Bangladesh for almost two years in 2000 and 2001.
36. Davis, "Planet of Slums."
37. E. Cline, *Overdressed: The Shockingly High Cost of Cheap Fashion*, New York: Portfolio, 2012.
38. N. Kauffman, "More and More U.S. Clothes Are Made by Bangladeshi Workers Earning Pennies an Hour," *Hartford Courant*, May 10, 2013; Office of the United States Trade Representative, Bangladesh, https://ustr.gov/countries-regions/south-central-asia/Bangladesh.
39. Bangladesh Garment Manufacturers and Exporters Association, "Factory Growth in BD," 2015, http://www.bgmea.com.bd/chart_test/factory_growth_in_bangladesh.
40. Bangladesh Garment Manufacturers and Exporters Association, "Product Export," 2011, http://www.bgmea.com.bd/chart_test/product_export.
41. Bangladesh Garment Manufacturers and Exporters Association, "Industry Strengths," 2011, http://www.bgmea.com.bd/home/about/Strengths.
42. Human Rights Watch, *Whoever Raises Their Heads*.
43. J. Hickel, "It's Time for a Global Minimum Wage," Al Jazeera, June 10, 2013, http://www.aljazeera.com.
44. Human Rights Watch, *Whoever Raises Their Heads*, 18.
45. Ibid., 21.
46. Unions in Bangladesh include the Bangladesh Federation for Workers Solidary and the Bangladesh Garments and Industrial Workers Federation. Human Rights Watch, *Whoever Raises Their Heads*.
47. Human Rights Watch, *Whoever Raises Their Heads*, 31.

48. Ibid., 21.
49. Popescu, *Bordering and Ordering*, 50.
50. Bangladesh Garment Manufacturers and Exporters Association, "Industry Strengths."
51. A. Escobar, *Encountering Development: The Making and Unmaking of the Third World*, Princeton, NJ: Princeton University Press, 1995.
52. *Last Week Tonight*, HBO, April 26, 2015; the story is available on YouTube, "Last Week Tonight with John Oliver: Fashion (HBO)," April 26, 2015.
53. J. Manik and N. Najar, "Bangladesh Police Charge 41 with Murder over Rana Plaza Collapse," *New York Times*, June 1, 2015.
54. Human Rights Watch, *Whoever Raises Their Heads*, 52.

7. Borders, Climate Change, and the Environment

1. United States National Park Service, *Effects of the International Boundary Pedestrian Fence in the Vicinity of Lukeville, Arizona on Drainage Systems and Infrastructure, Organ Pipe Cactus National Monument, Arizona*, nps.gov/orpi/learn/nature/upload/FloodReport_July2008_final.pdf, 2008.
2. J. Clark and M. Coppola, "Rainstorm Runoff Topples Border Fence, Floods Western Avenue," *Nogales International*, July 27, 2014, www.nogalesinternational.com.
3. Alliance for Global Justice, "Splitting the Land in Two: Ecological Effects of Border Militarization," 2013, https://afgj.org/splitting-the-land-in-two-ecological-effects-of-border-militarization.
4. I. Braverman, *Planting Flags: Trees, Land and Law in Israel–Palestine*, Cambridge, UK: Cambridge University Press, 2009.
5. A. Siddique, "Elephant Corridor through Indo–Bangla Border in Talks," *Dhaka Tribune*, February 17, 2016.
6. G. Hardin, "The Tragedy of the Commons," *Science* 162, 1968, 1,243–8.
7. E. Ostrom, *Governing the Commons: The Evolution of Institutions for Collective Action*, Cambridge, UK: Cambridge University Press, 1990; E. Ostrom, "Coping with Tragedies of the Commons," *Annual Review of Political Science* 2, 1999, 493–535; E. Ostrom, J. Burger, C. Field, R. Norgaard, and D. Policansky, "Revisiting the Commons: Local Lessons, Global Challenges," *Science* 284, 1999, 278–83.
8. J. Acheson, "Institutional Failure in Resource Management,"

Annual Review of Anthropology 35, 2006, 117–34; T. Sikor and C. Lund, "Access and Property: A Question of Power and Authority," *Development & Change* 40, 2009, 1–22.

9. C. Mora, S. Andréfouët, M. Costello, S. Kranenburg, A. Rollo, J. Veron, K. J. Gaston, and R. A. Myers, "Coral Reefs and the Global Network of Marine Protected Areas," *Science* 312, 2006, 1,750–1.

10. B. Mansfield, ed., *Privatization: Property and the Remaking of Nature-Society Relations,* London: Blackwell, 2008.

11. K. St. Martin, "The Difference That Class Makes: Neoliberalization and Non-Capitalism in the Fishing Industry of New England," in Mansfield, ed., *Privatization*, 133–55.

12. United Nations Food and Agricultural Organization, *State of World Fisheries and Aquaculture*, New York: FAO Fisheries Department, 2010.

13. W. Cronon, "The Trouble with Wilderness, or Getting Back to the Wrong Nature," in W. Cronon, ed., *Uncommon Ground: Rethinking the Human Place in Nature*, New York: W. W. Norton & Co., 1995, 69–90.

14. A Botswana government website explains: "In fact, hunting-gathering had become obsolete to sustain their living conditions. These agricultural land uses are not compatible with preserving wildlife resources and not sustainable to be practised in the Game Reserve." Government of Botswana, gov.bw.

15. N. Klein, *This Changes Everything: Capitalism vs the Climate,* New York: Simon & Schuster: New York, 2014, 169.

16. Intergovernmental Panel on Climate Change, *Fifth Assessment Report,* Geneva: Intergovernmental Panel Climate Change, 2013.

17. Ibid., 9. "The atmospheric concentrations of carbon dioxide, methane, and nitrous oxide have increased to levels unprecedented in at least the last 800,000 years. Carbon dioxide concentrations have increased by 40 percent since pre-industrial times, primarily from fossil fuel emissions and secondarily from net land use change emissions. The ocean has absorbed about 30 percent of the emitted anthropogenic carbon dioxide, causing ocean acidification."

18. E. Kolbert, *The Sixth Extinction: An Unnatural History*, New York: Henry Holt, 2014.

19. S. Henriques and K. Borowiecki, "The Drivers of Long-Run CO_2 Emissions: A Global Perspective since 1800," *EHES Working Papers in Economic History* 62, 2014, 1–45.

20. Measured in metric tons of carbon dioxide per person. US Energy Information Administration, eia.gov/countries.

21. A. Arnall, U. Kothari, and I. Kelman, "Introduction to Politics of

Climate Change: Discourses of Policy and Practice," *Geographical Journal* 180, 2014, 98–101.

22. J. Nevins, "Academic Jet-Setting in a Time of Climate Destabilization: Ecological Privilege and Professional Geographic Travel," *Professional Geographer* 66, 2014, 298–331, 303.

23. Intergovernmental Panel on Climate Change, *Fifth Assessment Report*.

24. M. Burkett, "A Justice Paradox: On Climate Change, Small Island Developing States, and the Quest for Effective Legal Remedy," *University of Hawaii Law Review* 35, 2013, 633.

25. Intergovernmental Panel on Climate Change, *Fifth Assessment Report*, chapter 29, p. 4 (1626).

26. Ibid., 15 (1627).

27. A. Baldwin, "Orientalizing Environmental Citizenship: Climate Change, Migration, and the Potentiality of Race," *Citizenship Studies* 16, 2012, 625–40; A. Baldwin, "Pluralising Climate Change and Migration: An Argument in Favour of Open Futures," *Geography Compass* 8, 2014, 516–28; M. Burkett, "Climate-Induced Migration: Is There a There There?" *Climate Law* 3, 2012, 3–14; K. McNamara and C. Gibson, "'We Do Not Want to Leave Our Land': Pacific Ambassadors at the United Nations Resist the Category of 'Climate Refugees,'" *Geoforum* 40, 2009, 475–83.

28. The efforts of the former Maldivian president Mohamed Nasheed to effect change at the 2009 UN climate talks in Copenhagen is detailed in the 2011 documentary *The Island President*.

29. Klein, *This Changes Everything*, 259.

30. Ibid., 276.

31. Murphy, "Sovereign State System as Political-Territorial Ideal."

32. R. Byrd, *The Senate, 1789–1889: Classic Speeches, 1830–1993*, Washington, DC: Government Printing Office, 1994.

33. M. Bradbury, *Becoming Somaliland: Reconstructing a Failed State*, Bloomington: Indiana University Press, 2008.

34. United Nations Conference on Environment and Development, 1992, Rio Declaration on Environment and Development, http://www.unep.org/Documents.Multilingual/Default.asp?documentid=78&articleid=1163.

35. Ibid.

36. Ibid.

37. European Environment Agency, "Total Greenhouse Gas (GHG) Emission Trends and Projections, October 22, 2014, http://www.eea.europa.eu/data-and-maps/indicators/greenhouse-gas-emission-trends-5/assessment-1.

38. United States Senate, 105th Congress, 1st session, July 25, 1997, roll call, http://www.senate.gov/legislative/LIS/roll_call_lists/roll_call_vote_cfm.cfm?congress=105&session=1&vote=00205.

39. Data is available at the United Nations Framework Convention on Climate Change website: unfccc.int.

40. United Nations Environment and Development, *The Lima Call for Climate Action*, 2014, http://newsroom.unfccc.int/lima/lima-call-for-climate-action-puts-world-on-track-to-paris-2015/#downloads.

41. R. Harrabin, "After Copenhagen," BBC News, December 19, 2009.

42. G. Low, "How the Lima Climate Change Talks Failed," *Telegraph*, December 15, 2014.

43. Harrabin, "After Copenhagen."

44. B. Obama, "Statement by the President on the Paris Climate Agreement," December 12, 2015, https://www.whitehouse.gov.

45. O. Milman, "James Hansen, Father of Climate Change Awareness, Calls Paris Talks 'a Fraud,'" *Guardian*, December 12, 2015.

46. T. Phillips, "China Underreporting Coal Consumptions by Up to 17%, Data Suggests," *Guardian*, November 4, 2015.

47. G. Cumming, D. Cumming, H. David, and C. Redman, "Scale Mismatches in Social-Ecological Systems: Causes, Consequences, and Solutions," *Ecology and Society* 11, 2006, 1–20.

48. N. Heynen, J. McCarthy, S. Prudham, and P. Robbins, *Neoliberal Environments: False Promises and Unnatural Consequences*, New York: Routledge, 2007.

49. Nevins, "Academic Jet-Setting," 304.

Conclusion: Movement as a Political Act

1. W. Connor, "The Impact of Homeland on Diasporas," in G. Sheffer, ed., *Modern Diasporas in International Politics*, New York: St. Martin's Press, 1986; R. Kaiser, "Homeland Making and the Territorialization of National Identity," in D. Conversi, ed., *Ethnonationalism in the Contemporary World: Walker Connor and the Study of Nationalism*, New York: Routledge, 2002, 229–47; R. Kaiser, "Fatherland/Homeland," in *The International Encyclopedia of Human Geography*, London: Elsevier, 2009.

2. J. Agnew, *Place and Politics: The Geographical Mediation of State and Society*, Boston: Allen and Unwin, 1987; Y. F. Tuan, *Space and Place: The Perspective of Experience*, Minneapolis: University of

Minnesota Press, 2001.

3. M. Billig, *Banal Nationalism*, Thousand Oaks, CA: Sage, 1995; T. Edensor, *National Identity, Popular Culture and Everyday Life*, Oxford: Berg, 2002.

4. Anderson, *Imagined Communities*, 1991; R. Brubaker, *Nationalism Reframed: Nationhood and the National Question in the New Europe*, Cambridge, UK: Cambridge University Press, 1996; R. Brubaker, "Manichean Myth"; R. Brubaker, "Ethnicity without Groups," *European Journal of Sociology* 43, 2002, 163–89; R. Brubaker and F. Cooper, "Beyond Identity," *Theory and Society* 29, 2000, 1–47; R. Brubaker, M. Loveman, and P. Stamatov, "Ethnicity as Cognition," *Theory and Society* 33, 2004, 31–64; E. Gellner, *Nations and Nationalism*, Oxford: Blackwell, 1983.

5. New archeological research is beginning to fill in some of these gaps with evidence of rich cultural and traditions in Central Asian nomadic communities. See J. Wilford, "Artifacts Show Sophistication of Ancient Nomads," *New York Times*, March 12, 2012.

6. Creswell, "On the Move," 20.

7. Mann, *States, War and Capitalism*, 1988; M. Weber, "Politics as a Vocation," in D. Owen and T. Strong, eds., *The Vocation Lectures*, Indianapolis, IN: Hackett Books, 2004.

8. G. Agamben, *Homo Sacer: Sovereign Power and Bare Life*, Stanford, CT: Stanford University Press, 1998; G. Agamben, *State of Exception*, Chicago: University of Chicago Press, 2005; C. Schmitt, *The Concept of the Political*, Chicago: University of Chicago Press, 1996.

9. B. Jessop, *The Capitalist State: Marxist Theories and Methods*, Oxford: Martin Robertson, 1982.

10. Many scholars have analyzed the relationship between neoliberalism, globalization, and capitalism. For instance, Harvey, *New Imperialism*.

11. I. Abraham and W. van Schendel, *Illicit Flows and Criminal Things: States, Borders, and the Other Side of Globalization*, Bloomington: Indiana University Press, 2005.

12. Mezzadra and Neilson, *Border as Method*.

13. A. Abbott, "Things of Boundaries," *Social Research* 62, 1995, 857–82, 857.

14. Brubaker, "Ethnicity without Groups," 164.

15. M. Dathan, "David Cameron Announces New Crackdown on Non-EU Immigration," *Guardian*, June 10, 2015.

16. Quoted in *Russia Today*, "Le Pen Compares Migrant Influx to Barbarian Invasion of Rome," September 16, 2015, https://www.rt.com/news/315466-le-pen-migrant-barbarian-invasion.

17. M. Day, "Europe 'Doesn't Give a Damn' about Immigration Quotas," *Independent,* June 15, 2015.
18. M. Eddy, "Anti-Immigrant Party Gains in Demark Elections," *New York Times,* June 18, 2015.
19. D. Bilefsky, "Denmark's New Front in Debate over Immigrants: Children's Lunches," *New York Times,* January 20, 2016.
20. Brian and Laczko, *Fatal Journeys,* 164.
21. N. Onishi, "South African Army Deployed in Areas Hit by Anti-Immigrant Violence," *New York Times,* April 21, 2015.
22. A. Ahmed and P. Villegas, "Dominican Republic Set to Deport Haitian Migrants," *New York Times,* June 17, 2015.
23. S. Springer, "Human Geography without Hierarchy," *Progress in Human Geography* 38, 2014, 402–19; S. Springer, "Why a Radical Geography Must Be Anarchist," *Dialogues in Human Geography* 4, 2014, 249–70.
24. Nevins, "Policing Mobility," 25.
25. B. Anderson, N. Sharma, and C. Wright, "Editorial: Why No Borders?" *Refuge* 26, 2009, 5–18; A. Buchanan and M. Moore, eds., *States, Nations, and Borders: The Ethics of Making Boundaries,* Cambridge, UK: Cambridge University Press, 2003; J. Carens, "Aliens and Citizens: The Case for Open Borders," *Review of Politics* 49, 1987, 251–73; J. Carens, *The Ethics of Immigration,* Oxford: Oxford University Press, 2013; S. Farris, "Homelands: The Case for Open Immigration," *Deca Stories,* 2014; M. Huemer, "Is There a Right to Immigrate?" *Social Theory and Practice* 36, 2010, 429–61; Walia, *Undoing Border Imperialism*; R. G. Wright, "Federal Immigration Law and the Case for Open Entry," *Loyola Law Review* 27, 1991, 1,265–98.
26. Carens, "Aliens and Citizens."
27. Universal Declaration of Human Rights: http://www.un.org/en/documents/udhr.
28. Carens, "Aliens and Citizens."
29. The right to free movement within a country is not even as absolute as it first appears. While it is possible to travel all the way across the United States or the European Union without encountering a border checkpoint, it is not possible to make that trip along any route you choose or along the most direct path between two places. Instead, movement is restricted within states through the idea of private property. To go to the store, an individual does not select the most direct route, because that would involve cutting through your neighbor's yard, jumping over strangers' fences, and cutting through the properties of private businesses. Our movements within states are more restricted than we generally perceive.

30. The provisions easing mobility have not, however, led to a much higher occurrence of mobility within the European Union. Only about 2 percent of EU citizens live and work in another EU member state. This figure has remained stable for about thirty years, and even the EU eastward enlargement has had little effect on it. See Bundeszentrale für Politische Bildung, "EU Internal Migration Before and During the Economic and Financial Crisis— An Overview," March 22, 2013, bpb.de/gesellschaft/migration/ kurzdossiers/157035/eu-internal-migration?p=all.

31 The website openborders.info serves as a clearinghouse for information on the idea of open borders.

32. D. Laitin and M. Jahr, "Let Syrians Settle Detroit," *New York Times*, May 14, 2015; P. Legrain, "Open Up, Europe! Let Migrants In," *New York Times,* May 6, 2015.

33. Huemer, "Is There a Right to Migrate?"; Wright, "Federal Immigration Law."

34. Hickel, "It's Time for a Minimum Wage"; M. Yunus, "After the Savar Tragedy, Time for an International Minimum Wage," *Guardian,* May 12, 2013. The organization International Convention for a Global Minimum Wage is mobilizing for a minimum wage; see http://www.international-convention-for-minimum-wage.org.

35. J. Schmitt, *Why Does the Minimum Wage Have No Discernable Effect on Employment?* New York: Center for Economic Policy, 2013.

36. All of these hours would not necessarily be made up. There are also questions about whether enough skilled workers could be found to continue production.

37. G. Deleuze and F. Guattari, *A Thousand Plateaus,* Minneapolis: University of Minnesota Press, 1987, 23.

38. M. de Certeau, *The Practice of Everyday Life,* Berkeley: University of California Press, 1984.

39. J. Ferguson, *The Anti-Politics Machine*, Minneapolis: University of Minnesota Press, 1994.

40. S. Springer, "Why a Radical Geography Must Be Anarchist," 2014, 260.

Index